On Your Marks!

A practical guide to mark making, early writing and language

LE3028

ISBN: 978-1-903670-97-2

© Michael Jones

Photographs © Michael Jones

All rights reserved

First published 2016

Printed in the UK for Lawrence Educational
PO Box 532, Cambridge, CB1 0BX, UK

Acknowledgements

All the practical activities in this book have been tried and tested with children. Many have been recommended by practitioners and advisors across the UK. Special thanks go to Kelly Yuen, Debbie Brace, Tina Cooke, Mary Field, Abbie Rainbow-Dias, Frances Turnbull, Barbara Bourn, Katie Monastero and Claire Blanchard.

Thank you also to the following settings who provided inspiration: Shortstown Preschool, Bedford; Sacred Heart Primary School, Luton; St Joseph's Catholic Primary School, Luton; Millington Road Nursery School, Cambridge; Woodlands Nursery and Infant School, Solihull; East Thurrock Kids Club, Stanford-le-Hope; Smarteez Neighbourhood Nursery, Bedford; Kilkeel Nursery School, Newry; Puddleducks Nursery, Bedford; Gateway Academy Westminster; and Ecole Maternelle, St-Hilaire-la-Palud, France.

The author royalties from the sale of this book will be donated to the playgroup at Kep Gardens, Kep Province, Cambodia, an education cer children living on the edge of a forest. For details of this wonderful organisation please visit www.kepgardens.com

Permission to photocopy

Contents

Introduction

What is 'mark making'?

Mark making is a term used to describe how children make marks on different surfaces, including paper. Mark making in early years develops into early letter and number formation, i.e. *handwriting*.

How does mark making develop into writing?

Children begin mark making accidentally and randomly when they are babies, e.g. smearing their food on their highchair tray. With time, making marks becomes something they do on purpose. With encouragement, children learn to make simple marks such as hand prints or to use finger paints to dab spots onto paper. With adult support and by copying other children, they learn to make shapes, e.g. lines, crosses and circles, and patterns such as zigzags. As they grow physically, children become more able to hold and use various tools for painting, drawing and writing. Children develop their skills as they gain more experience, particularly with help and encouragement from adults. Their ability to see patterns around them and create them through making marks increases too. As children develop in their understanding of reading they learn that certain marks we make are called 'writing'. This understanding leads them to experiment with writing recognisable letters, words and numbers in the language that they are being brought up in.

Who is this book for?

This book is for anyone working with children between the ages of two and five years, or with older children with additional learning needs. The ideas can be shared with parents as a way of helping them understand what you are aiming to achieve. This will help to involve them in developing their children's mark making and early writing at home.

Terminology

In this book we call anyone who works with young children an 'adult' and the place where they work with children a 'setting'. To make the book easier to read, we refer to children as 'he' and anything used to paint, draw or write with as a 'tool'. We refer to children from two to three and a half years of age, who are developing their language and exploring gross- and fine-motor skills, as 'very young children'. This can also include older children with significant additional learning needs. 'Older children' are from age three years six months onwards, who have well-developed language and are often ready to develop fine-motor skills specifically related to early writing. Those looking after children at home are called 'parents'.

Some technical words and phrases are shown in italics within the text. For easy reference, these are explained in the glossary at the back of the book.

How to use this book

This book has a mix of explanation, advice and practical ideas. You can use it to help you decide how you are going to approach mark making and early writing in your setting, or to improve or change what you already do. The Important Ideas section gives background information about why mark making is vital for writing. Some pages with practical ideas have suggested vocabulary that you might want to introduce to children as you are talking and playing with them. This will help children to understand mark making and writing and to express their own ideas.

Important Ideas

Making marks, making sense and talking

Mark making and speech and language development go hand in hand. Children learn to talk because they understand that people can use spoken sounds and words to represent objects and ideas. They know that when someone says, 'dog' it can mean a real dog, a toy dog or a picture of a dog. When children begin to talk, they use speech sounds to make up words. In the same way, children learn that what they paint, draw or write can stand for something real, e.g. a picture of themselves and eventually writing their own name.

Children learn to talk naturally as part of being involved in play and conversations. However, many of the skills involved in mark making need to be taught, and particularly writing letter shapes and numbers. Children learn new things when they are involved in activities that make sense. This is particularly true of learning how to write. If children take part in activities that are meaningful and fun, they will want to be involved in them again and again. This helps them increase and improve their physical skills and understanding of what writing is for.

Adults and children talking together

How adults talk with children when they are mark making is just as important as what the children actually do. For example, adults might say, 'That's a lovely painting. I can see a circle there.' Or 'I like your drawing of lots of people. Is one of them you?' Or, 'Oh! I can see that the person you have drawn has got two arms and five fingers! What about his legs?' Or, 'What are you writing? Oh, it's your name! Of course it is! I can see you have written T for Tom lots of times.' These types of comments and responses give children the vocabulary to describe what they are doing, as well as confidence as mark makers and early writers.

Children working towards handwriting

Hopefully, the end product of mark making is a child who loves to pick up a pencil and knows how to write letters, words and numbers quickly, effortlessly and without thinking about what he is doing with his hands. Then he can concentrate on what he is going to write about, rather than the physical effort of writing. Other people will be able to read and enjoy what he has written because they can read his lovely handwriting! Everything we do during mark-making activities works towards the child being able to use a pencil to write, using what is known as a *dynamic tripod grasp* or *tripod grasp*. This is the accepted 'correct' way for children to hold a pencil in the UK. By the time children are seven years old, they have usually reached the stage where they can automatically use a pencil correctly.

Learning to write is a whole-body experience

Learning to write involves much more than concentrating on our preferred hand and our fingers. As babies become able to sit up and stand they develop stability in their shoulders, while at the same time gradually developing strength and control over their arms, wrists, hands and fingers. This allows them first to reach for, pick up and handle relatively large objects with both hands, e.g. a cup or teddy bear. With the development of their brains, nervous systems and muscles, they become able to pick up very small objects between their fingers and thumb.

Throughout the early years and first years of school, children are developing strength and control of *gross-motor movements* and *fine-motor movements.* They also develop *hand-eye coordination,* where they are able to look at something, reach out and hold it and watch what they are doing. Eventually, they do this automatically – without thinking. Very young children, between 18 months and three years, might not have the

strength or control to hold a small pencil or to be able to keep their shoulders or wrists steady. You will see them grasp a chunky crayon in their fist and make big, whole arm movements. For this reason it is important to match the right type of mark-making tool to the child's particular stage of physical development, e.g. giving thick, chunky crayons to younger children and thin pencils as well for those who are older.

Developing children's upper-body strength and control, including in their shoulders and arms, is essential for mark making and early writing. Their *posture,* how they stand, crouch or sit in a balanced, comfortable and relaxed way, is also important. This gives children the stability they need to move their arms and hands freely and accurately, without needing to steady themselves or worry about losing their balance.

As children grow, they develop a sense of body awareness, or *proprioception*, so that they know where their bodies are in relation to other people and objects. This helps them to naturally adjust movements, e.g. to avoid bumping into other people or to reach down and pick up a crayon they have dropped on the floor. This information comes from the senses, and is transmitted to the brain so that they can make judgements about how to move. The sense of proprioception is essential for being able to move automatically, for being still and for planning to make a movement and then do it, i.e. to make movements in a conscious way.

Jumping, hopping, climbing and sliding all help posture and build strength, control and confidence in large movements.

The midline

The midline is an imaginary line that runs downwards from the centre of the top of your head and divides your body in two, so there are two equal and symmetrical halves. Many movements that we make involve us moving our arms across the midline; for example, reaching up with your right hand to pick up something that is on your left. Drawing some shapes and writing some letters involves crossing the midline. Young children find this quite difficult but as they grow it becomes easier and finally automatic. Here is an example: make a large 'x' in the air in front of you, using either your right or left hand. Point your finger straight ahead of you for the centre of the x. This is at the level of your midline. Now make a large x in the air in front of you. The first thing that you will have done is brought your hand up to the top left. As you brought it down to your bottom right, you have crossed your midline. Then you brought your hand up to the top right and moved it down to your bottom left. When you did this, you crossed your midline again.

Some older children with additional learning needs find crossing the midline very difficult, as do those with a movement difficulty known as *dyspraxia*. For this reason, physiotherapists and occupational therapists attach great importance to involving children in activities that include bringing their hands together at the midline, and consciously being able to cross the midline.

Automatic and planned movements

Children and adults make many movements *automatically*, without thinking. Some are *reflex actions* that don't involve any thinking, e.g. quickly moving your hand away when you have touched something hot. Other actions have been made so many times that we no longer need to think how to do them. For activities that involve very accurate gross-motor or fine-motor control, we need to think carefully before and while we are doing them, e.g. balancing on a beam or threading a needle. These *conscious* movements involve knowing how to make a movement, planning to do it, and being able to make that movement quickly, and most importantly, slowly and carefully.

Here's something you can do as an example of bringing automatic movements under conscious control. Pretend that you have a cactus plant and you touch the prickles with your finger quickly and without thinking. You almost certainly quickly moved your whole hand away, probably waved your hand around and perhaps then put your hurt finger in your mouth. You moved your hand away automatically, without thinking. Now pretend to touch the cactus again, but this time taking great care not to get hurt! You will have planned to move your finger towards the prickles very slowly, and then planned only to press just hard enough to feel that the prickles are, in fact, very prickly!

Very young children are learning about movement. They can make many movements automatically, but not when they think about them, and not slowly. These skills come with time and practice. This is also true about children learning to write, where we help them practise making precise movements, so that they eventually become automatic. It takes most children at least seven years to master the skills needed to write clearly, legibly and automatically.

Eventually, as children grow and gain experience, they increase their *manual dexterity*, or ability to move fingers to hold and manipulate tools and materials. This includes being able to consciously move each finger on its own. They will also be able to bring their thumb and *forefinger* together to pick up objects. This is known as the *pincer grasp*. From this point they will be able to learn to hold a pencil comfortably and begin to use it accurately.

Mark making and early writing is also about seeing, looking, hearing, listening, understanding, talking and making sense of what we are doing. So it is not just about holding a pencil, but is a whole mind and body experience!

Learning skills, practising skills and pretending to be a writer

Children want to learn how to paint, draw and write mainly because they see adults doing it. Writing is something that needs to be learned and children need to practise movements and experiment with some of the techniques. If children find activities appealing and easy to achieve, but with just the right amount of challenge, then they will want to do them again and again. For example, playing with dough can help many of the skills we have mentioned above. If adults regularly change the consistency, colour and texture of the dough, as well as the tools the children use, then children will get the stimulation, pleasure and practice that they need to develop their hand strength and fine-motor coordination. It also gives them the vocabulary they need to talk about *what* they are doing and *how* their hands feel.

Imitation and copying

There is an important difference between *imitation* and *copying*. Children imitate how adults and older children talk and behave. In mark making, this leads to pretending to be a writer *(role-play writing)*. Children naturally want to be just like adults and older children. A lot of their play involves pretending to be like other people and imitating what they do, including writing. Role-play writing also gives children the chance to practise many of the skills that they are starting to develop.

Copying, in mark making and early writing, refers to children being taught to make specific, accurate movements or marks, so that they can learn how to do something correctly. For example, we might show children how to put a brush back in a pot, or how to put their painting on a rack to dry. When they are ready, we might show them how to form an 'o' with a pencil, making a mark in the right direction or *orientation*. In these cases we would say to the child, 'Watch me' or, 'Do the same as me' or, 'Copy me'.

Copying also refers to *copy writing*, where children copy on top of, or underneath, what an adult has written; for example, copying their name. This is only really useful for older children, when an adult sits with them and talks them through what it is that they want them to copy. Older children enjoy copying activities, as long as they understand what they are supposed to be doing. Many children copy words that they see around them, particularly from wall displays. For this reason it is essential that adults write clearly, so that children always see accurate examples of how and what to write.

Children talking and mark making

Very young children

When two-year-olds decide that they are going to do something with their hands, such as mark making, they need to focus all their attention on the movements they are going to make. This includes concentrating on:
- how they hold mark-making tools
- how they use them to make marks (e.g. pressing hard enough)
- how they move the tools.

The adult's role is to help them with the tools and to give simple instructions, or make a simple running commentary, as you help the child to get organised. For example, you can sit or crouch quietly alongside the young child and make just a few comments. Once he has finished you might wait for him to say something, or comment on what he has done.

Example: Chris, the pot of water and the paintbrush

Chris is two years and six months old and is squatting down outside, trying to copy some older children who are busy dipping large brushes into small buckets and 'painting' the paving slabs.

Chris: 'Me want do it!'
Adult: 'Shall I help you dip your brush into the bucket?' (The adult steadies the bucket while Chris focuses on taking the brush out of the pot and putting it back in again. Chris squats down and happily paints away. The adult crouches next to him.)
Adult: 'In goes the brush. Out it comes. That's a lot of water!'
Chris: 'Lot of water. Splash! Me painting.'
Adult: 'Yes. There's a lot of water. You're having fun painting!'

Older children

Older children are more able to talk about what they are doing, while they are doing it. This is because many of their actions have become automatic. However, children from three to four years of age still need to focus carefully. A child can be easily distracted if adults ask him too many questions while he is concentrating. Children who are more experienced and confident about their skills can often have a conversation with either an adult or other children while they are busy painting or drawing. However, when it comes to practising writing skills, e.g. copying shapes or writing their name, they need to focus entirely on what they are doing with their hands. In this case, too much adult talk, other than simple comments, instructions or praise, can disturb their concentration.

Encouraging and praising children

Some things can be done just right, e.g. cutting in a straight line, putting the lid back on a felt-tipped pen or tidying up after cutting paper. We can praise children for this by saying, 'Well done!' because they finished the job or managed to do it correctly. (They have literally 'done it well'.) However, if a child has tried to do something, but has not got it quite right, it is better to say, 'Good try' or, 'You worked hard to get that right. Good try.'

For example, James, aged four, tries to write the letter J. He almost manages but his letter is orientated the wrong way. If we say, 'Well done!' James might think that he has formed his 'J' correctly. We could say, 'That's very good. You tried hard to make your J just right. That was a good try.' Then you might say, 'Shall I show you how to get it just right?' (The child agrees). 'We just need to turn it round a little bit. Look, watch me. Like that. Now you have a try.' The adult says, while James is writing: 'Down, curl it round. Stop. Now give it a hat. That's better. Your J is the right way round. Well done!'

Boys and girls

It is often said that girls are more interested in mark-making activities than boys, or that many boys are actually slower than girls to develop the skills needed for early writing. Rather than comparing girls and boys, I prefer to think about how we can make mark making and early writing exciting and meaningful for *all* children. Some children, for example, might be less interested in being involved in mark making, perhaps because many activities are pre-planned by adults, with children sitting at a table while the adult supervises them. In some children's minds, this means 'work'. If children are unsure of their fine-motor skills, but more confident about their gross-motor skills, then they are more likely to want to play

outside and less likely to want to sit down. Our job is to help these children enjoy making marks, while building their confidence in their fine-motor skills.

Sometimes adults expect more of girls and a lot less of boys. For example, we generally expect girls to be more able at self-help skills at a younger age than boys. Children develop many fine-motor skills through learning to get dressed and undressed. If we expect boys to be less able to get dressed, then we will be more likely to dress them ourselves. As a result the boys miss out on developing their fine-motor skills and hand-eye coordination.

If children prefer to spend time exploring and moving around outside, then our challenge is to develop activities outdoors that involve mark making. These should be part of activities that children already enjoy, e.g. riding on tricycles. For example, if we involve children in washing the tricycles and cars and squeezing out sponges while they are doing it, this makes perfect sense and is great fun. As a result the children will want to do this activity regularly. Without realising it, they will be practising important skills and developing the strength needed for mark making. You could also ask children to paint road markings on the playground to make a road. These types of activities help make mark making appealing to all children. As a result, their confidence grows, so they will want to take part in more mark-making activities, indoors and out.

When children have difficulties

Most children develop all the skills and confidence they need for early writing by taking part in the types of activities described in this book. However, some children show from an early age that they will need support. A small minority might have been put off mark making because they have been introduced to writing too early.

Avoiding mark making

In general, children in early years choose to take part in activities that appeal to them and that they know they will be able to master. Children also tend to avoid activities that they think will be difficult. Some children will rarely get involved in mark making, and particularly early writing activities because they sense that it will be difficult. This is often because the children are less confident about their fine-motor skills or hand-eye coordination. As a result, they spend a lot of time doing what is easy for them, which is usually taking part in activities with a lot of gross-motor movement, e.g. playing on the bikes outside. Because they don't practise fine-motor skills they may lack the strength and skills needed for early writing.

Fear of writing

Some children develop a fear of adult-led activities involving sitting at a table and picking up a pen or pencil to write. This is often because they have been introduced to writing their name before they were ready, or they have additional difficulties that make fine-motor control challenging. Some parents mistakenly believe that their children should be taught to write their name at a very young age.

Speech and language difficulties

Children with delayed speech and language can develop problems with reading and writing when they are older. They are unsure how speech sounds can be joined together to make words, or how words can be used to express ideas. In the same way, they are unsure how writing is made up of letters and words to express meaning.

Being able to pronounce words clearly involves the coordination of many muscles. Some children have speech (pronunciation) difficulties

because they have problems with all fine-motor movements in general. This also shows itself by having difficulties with the hand-eye coordination and fine-motor skills needed to hold a paintbrush or pen and make it do what the child wants. Some children with severe speech difficulties might be showing early signs of *dyslexia*. This can include difficulties with being able to recognise patterns and sequences (see page 25 *Patterns*).

Other difficulties

Children with *global developmental disability,* such as *Down syndrome,* are likely to need extra support with fine-motor coordination. Children with *dyspraxia* often have speech (pronunciation) difficulties, where they can only make sounds and say words easily when they are not thinking about them. In the same way, they are able to make automatic movements, without thinking, but can't make the same movements when they plan to do them, or when an adult asks them to do them.

All of the activities in this book are helpful for children with additional learning needs. These help children overcome their worries about using their hands to enjoy practising fine-motor movements and making marks. It is essential to seek advice. Practical ideas and help given by speech and language therapists, occupational therapists, physiotherapists and special needs advisors can be introduced in the setting for the benefit of all children.

So let's explore mark making and early writing!

Paper

Key ideas

Most of the marks that children make will be on paper. There are many types of paper, so it is important to decide what paper/card will be freely available for children to use and what will be stored for special activities when adults are joining in with children. Put trays of special paper and card out of children's reach but where they can see them. Children can use these items but only when an adult is supervising. This helps children to understand the value of paper and card, and encourages adults to plan to be available to support children in their mark making!

Talking accurately about what things are called and what they look like is important for children's vocabulary development. The following list includes only some of the types of paper you might use.

Card is a type of thick paper that often comes in A4 sheets. It is relatively easy to cut.

Cardboard is what boxes are made out of. It is much thicker than card. Cardboard is great for making large constructions together and painting. It is very difficult to cut with scissors.

Newsprint paper (often called fish and chip paper) usually comes in large sheets from an educational supplier. It is very thin and is mainly used for painting on. It tends to tear when children write with sharp pencils or felt-tipped pens, so it can be frustrating for them to write on.

Lining paper is a type of wallpaper that is used in home decorating for covering a wall before you paint. It comes in rolls and is available from DIY stores. It is not cheap but is ideal for covering tables and rolling onto the floor so that children can draw, paint and write together with most types of tool.

Photocopy paper is ideal for writing on and cutting.

Sugar paper is soft and comes in large sheets or rolls. It can be used as backing paper for displays. Black sugar paper is ideal for use with chalks. White sugar paper is ideal for painting on.

Wallpaper offcuts are often used by practitioners for children to paint on. If children paint on the reverse side of embossed paper, then they can see exciting patterns. However, many wallpapers are shiny on the back and paint can take a long time to dry. They are not good for writing on as the ridges can be very frustrating.

Paper is very expensive! It is good to use recycled paper for children to practise writing on. This gives children an important message about recycling. However, if you are planning to put children's mark making on display, then it is best to use good quality paper (see page 5 *Displays*). Local printers are usually very happy to supply you with offcuts of good-quality paper and card. These can then be cut up in different sizes and shapes to make the paper more appealing to children (see page 38 *Making Books*).

Pens and Other Mark-Making Tools

Key ideas

There are many types of writing tools and they all have different names. It is important that children know the right names for tools, so whenever you talk with children about their mark making use the correct vocabulary. Pens, pencils and felt-tipped pens are expensive. Help children value the tools they use by showing them regularly how to use and care for them. Keep different types of pens in separate tubs or attractive boxes so children can find and tidy them up easily.

In the descriptions of tools below, the key vocabulary is italicised to show just how much there is to talk about. The conversations that you have about how to use and care for writing tools can be just as rich as talking about the marks that children make!

Pencils should be *sharp* and *sharpened* with a *pencil sharpener*. You can make patterns with the *shavings* from *coloured pencils*. At home you can keep your pens and pencils and felt-tipped pens in *a pencil case.*

Writing and drawing pencils have a *lead* in the middle. If you want to change what you have drawn or written then you can rub it out with a *rubber*. You can't rub out what you have drawn with a coloured pencil. Some pencils are *short* and *stubby,* which helps very young children to hold and grip them comfortably.

Felt-tipped pens or **felt pens** are often *valuable* and *expensive* so they need to be *looked after* very carefully. A felt pen has a *lid* or *top*. When you *take off* the lid, you can put it on the other end of the pen so you don't *lose* it. When you have *finished* using it, don't forget to put the lid *back on* otherwise the felt pen will *dry out*. This would be a *shame*. Some felt pens are very *special*. **Magic pens** are very exciting because you can draw or write with one colour and then use the *clear* pen to write on top – and your writing will change colour! Note: If you dip the end of a *dried-out* felt pen in water this might be enough to bring it back to life.

Marker pens are usually *short* and *thick* and have a thick felt end for writing and drawing. They are designed to be used by adults on flip charts and whiteboards. Note: It is very important to use only marker pens designed for children, as adult pens with permanent ink can stain children's clothing or skin. Some whiteboard markers contain alcohol and give off fumes. The *felt-tipped* ends of marker pens are often *rounded*. Some marker pens have *chisel tips*.

Crayons or **wax crayons** are usually *short* and *thin* or *stubby*. This makes them ideal for very young children to hold, and for making big movements when creating shapes and patterns, or for drawing and *scribbling*. If you use wax crayons on lining paper and then paint over the wax with a thin mixture of powder paint and water, you can create an exciting effect that highlights the colour of the wax. This makes an attractive backing paper for wall displays.

Mark-Making Areas

Key ideas

Many settings have a separate area for mark making. This is a good idea but only as long as adults plan to be in the area. During those times, adults can talk and play with the children, make displays and show them how to use various resources.

A mark-making area should be as near as possible to where children spend most of their time reading and sharing books. This encourages children to bring books into the mark-making area and to take mark-making resources into the book area. If the book area has a table and chairs in it children will be much more likely to draw and write there.

Resources for a mark-making area

The table and chairs that you put in the area are the most important starting point. Children are often attracted to a space that has a table and chairs they and an adult can sit comfortably in for a long time.

As well as having various types of paper, pens, scissors and glue sticks available, it is useful for adults to set up different small activities in the area. Spend time playing with these activities with the children. This can include making envelopes and writing letters to go inside them, and making and writing books (see page 38 *Making Books*). A key resource is a small display nearby with a photograph of each child with their name below. Another box with the children's name cards should be within easy reach, so that children can find their own name and other children's if they need them. This helps them with their *developmental/emergent writing* (see page 29 *Developmental Writing*).

It is helpful to have materials stored nearby, perhaps with drawers that are clearly labelled and with a photo of what is in the drawer. This helps children to find what they want, read what it is called and hopefully put it back in the right place when they have finished! Any writing tools that the children use should be checked daily to make sure that they are in good condition.

Naming the area

I prefer 'writing area'. Then you can say to children, 'Come and do some writing.' If you call it a 'mark-making area' then children will not know what you mean when you say, 'Come and do some mark making.' If you decide to put up a big sign nearby, it can be helpful to write a caption with the words 'write' or 'writing' in it, e.g. 'Come and do some drawing and writing!' or 'Come and draw and write!'

Practitioners may be worried that if the area focuses mainly on early writing, then only children who can already write will go there. One way of encouraging all sorts of mark-making activities in the area is to regularly provide items like scissors, glue, rulers and different types of paper and mark-making tools, so that children feel that they can draw and cut and stick too.

Examples of Mark-Making Areas

Key ideas

This setting's mark-making area was next to the book area. Children could help themselves to the resources that they needed from the drawers. The whole area was quite 'business-like', but this attracted children who were keen to cut and stick and draw, and pretend to be writers.

This setting had very limited space so made their writing area near the book area and right next to where the staff made their notes and stored the children's files! This encouraged the children to pretend to be writers. The adults and children set the area up together and the children decided that they wanted to have the same resources as the manager: sticky notes, a stapler and pencils and pens in a mug!

Displays

Key ideas

Attractive displays of children's mark making help children regularly talk about mark making with practitioners, with other children and with their parents. Take photographs of children while they are busy mark making and display these with the children's pictures and writing. Children tend not to look up, so it is good to have displays at children's eye level, so adults and children can talk together about what they have done. Displays that are popular and exciting will get touched a lot! I recommend covering them with large sheets of acetate.

Sometimes what we write on displays can be just as important as the children's work. Avoid using complicated technical language. For example, a display with a title 'Developing fine-motor skills to promote mark making' might be accurate but is likely to be confusing and off-putting for parents. On the other hand, 'Squeezing dough makes our fingers strong and will help us to hold a pencil!' is accurate, appealing, interesting and fun to read.

Children love to be reminded of what they were talking about when they were making marks. Parents like to read this too! With each child's painting, add a speech bubble with what the child was saying. For example, 'This is my mummy.'

Take a photo of the child while he is painting. Add a speech bubble and write down what he said when he was busy doing the activity, e.g. 'I am making a round shape in the paint with my finger.' Display the speech bubble with the photo.

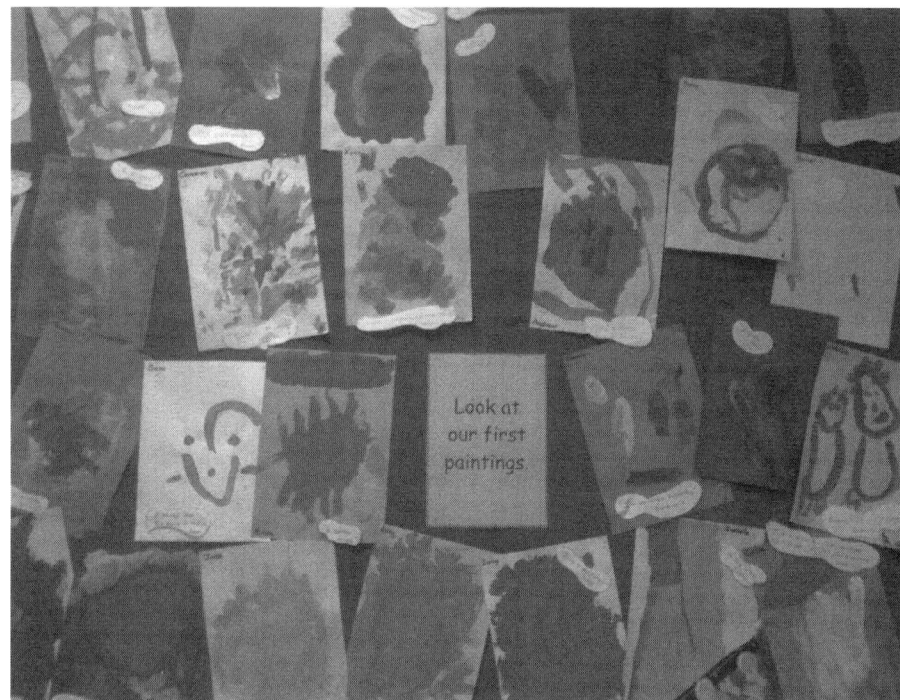

Important point: It can be tempting only to display pictures that resemble what they are supposed to be, or mark making that actually looks like writing. In many settings, practitioners make a point of displaying everyone's work. This gives the important message that everyone can make marks and that children are at different stages of development.

Painting

Key ideas

Most children love painting. Regular painting activities enable children to practise important skills and build the knowledge they need to form the foundations for writing. This is particularly true when adults are involved with helping children to prepare for painting, talking about what they are doing and tidying up afterwards. Painting is a creative activity and if adults can be with children while they are painting, there is huge potential for children to develop their language. Painting also helps children make accurate movements, e.g. taking a brush out of a pot, using it and then putting the brush carefully back into the pot they took it from.

Different types of painting activities develop different skills:

Painting at an easel strengthens children's shoulders as they reach up towards the paper. It also helps develop children's sense of balance, so that they can stand still and move their shoulders, arms and hands to put the paint in exactly the place where they want it to go. Painting at an easel is particularly important for helping children to make movements where they will cross their midline (see page vi).

Painting at a table or on the floor on large sheets of paper encourages children to paint together, so they talk with, copy and learn from each other. Rolls of lining paper are particularly useful for covering tables or making a large space on the floor for children to paint. Using masking tape is the best way to stick the paper to a table or the floor.

Encourage the children to help you cover the table. This involves cutting the paper to size and sticking the masking tape in place, all of which develop fine-motor skills. Begin the activity with only a few chairs round the table, as this may encourage the children to move around, paint and talk with each other. Younger children might prefer to stand as it is easier for them to reach for the paints and make big movements with the tools.

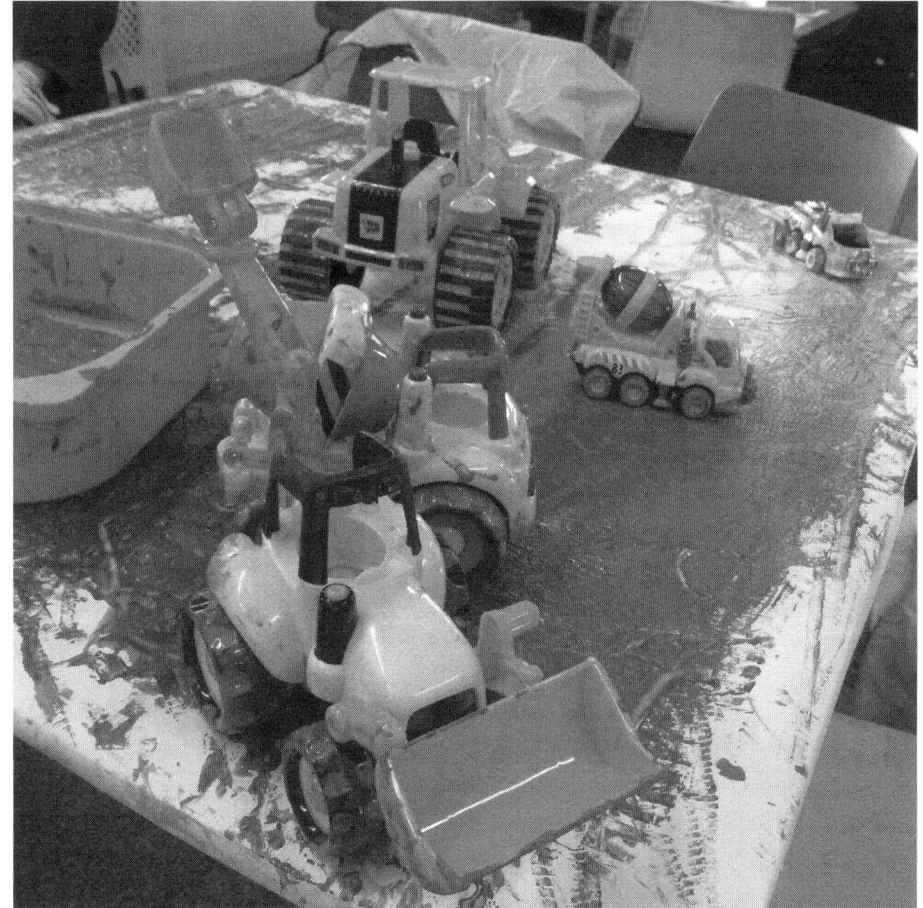

Two-year-olds had great fun painting the wheels of these lorries and diggers and moving them around on the paper.

Preparing for Painting – and Tidying Up!

Key ideas

Helping children to get organised before and after painting can provide many opportunities for talking and learning. Putting on and taking off an apron, washing hands and clearing up spills involve many coordinated movements and a lot of talking!

Aprons

Help children by having aprons hung in such a way that they can easily choose the apron they need and put it back afterwards. A series of four hooks or pegs, with an apron on each, will be easier for children to manage than several aprons on one hook.

Hand washing

It may be more convenient to send children to the sinks or basins to wash their hands after they have finished painting, but having a bowl of water on a table nearby with soap, a nailbrush and a towel, gives children a lot to talk about. You will also need to provide a cloth to wipe the table, a floor cloth and a scrubbing brush to clean up spills. It will be essential for an adult to be nearby to supervise children and to get involved in conversation.

Paint brushes

Different types of paintbrush not only produce different marks but also encourage children to learn and use different words. Children tend to use brushes that they can grip and use easily, so it is important to make sure that you have different types of brushes in the setting.

Very young children, for example, prefer short, thick brushes because they can hold them easily in the palm of their hand. They will make thick brushstrokes or dab with the brush.

Older children are more skilled at using longer, thinner brushes, using a grip similar to a mature pencil grip. This helps them to make more detailed paintings. As a result, they often have more to talk about!

Specialist brushes can encourage deep concentration and careful movements. Some specialist brushes, such as the one in the photo below, are designed like felt-tipped pens but have paint in the barrel and a brush end. They encourage fine movements and a grip similar to a mature pencil grip (see page 22) so are more likely to appeal to older children. Specialist brushes can be expensive and need to be used in a particular way to get the best results. It is important for adults to stay with the children, to show them how to use and care for the brushes, and to talk with the children about what they are doing and what they have done.

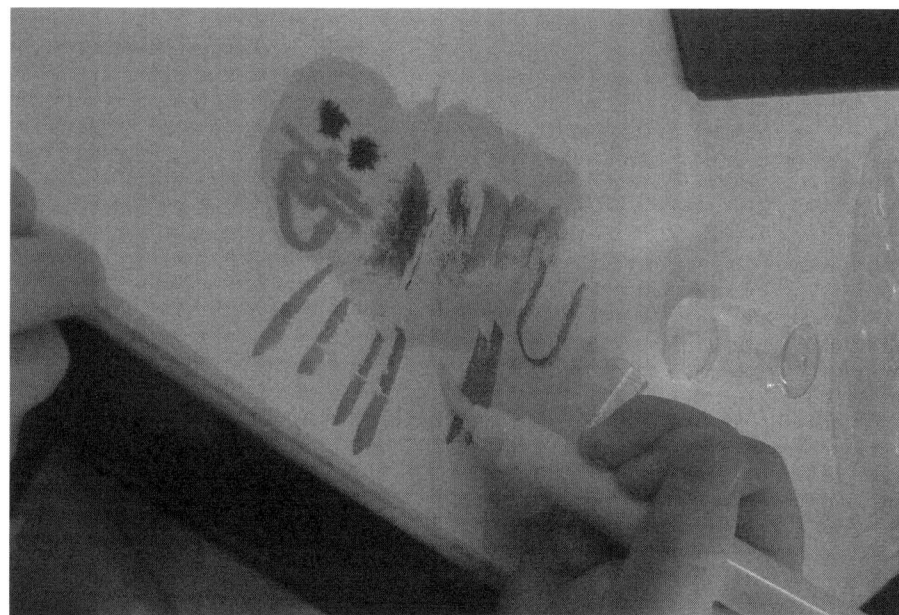

Mixing Paint and Finger Painting

Key ideas and activities

There are many types of paint, from powder paint that you mix with water and ready-mixed paint in squeezy plastic bottles to small, round, hard blocks of paint to which you gradually add water to make water colours. Each type of paint prompts different reactions and language from the children, different types of marks and finished results. Preparing paints with children before they start and while they are painting produces a great deal of stimulating conversation and gives the adults the chance to show children how to use the paints and tools.

Choosing and mixing colours encourages lots of talk: about individual colours, what might happen when you mix colours together, the shapes you made while you were mixing and what colour you ended up with!

Finger painting

This is very messy, exciting and satisfying for children and adults alike! Of all the painting activities this is the one that will probably generate most talk: about hands and fingers, what we can do with them and how they feel. Mix up finger paint on a table top with the children, adding various amounts of water to make it more or less runny. Encourage children to use both hands to make circular movements with their whole hand, or to make shapes with one finger at a time. If you have another table nearby covered in blank paper, then children can make hand prints, shapes and even write with their paint-covered fingers. Adding different ingredients to the paint, e.g. small amounts of fine sand or glitter, creates different textures and gives children more to feel and talk about.

Some children really do not like getting their hands dirty or might have very sensitive skin. Experiment with allowing them to use thin gloves. If they still don't like finger painting then try giving them a tray with paint on and stretch a large sheet of cling film over it so they are not actually touching the paint itself.

To save the shapes and patterns that the children have made, place a piece of white paper over the paint and carefully peel it away. Once the paper has dried it can be added to a display about finger painting.

Suggested vocabulary

Strokes; dabbing; splodge; lines; spots; more paint; too much; painting from top to bottom; side-to-side; carefully; wet; runny; thick; squeeze hard; gently.

Painting and Mark Making Outdoors

Key ideas

Bad weather often makes it impractical to use paper outdoors. However, it can be very exciting to involve the children in rolling out a large length of lining paper and weighting it down with large pieces of wood and heavy stones. Children can make very different marks if there are several types of brushes or rollers available. They can drip paint, smear it, or even walk on the paper and make marks with rubber boots. When they have finished, they can have fun walking in a builders' tray of water until they have got their boots clean. Cleaning the ground afterwards with scrubbing brushes and a watering can filled with soapy water, adds extra interest to the activity and encourages big movements that develop the children's strength. An adult can help children use a large yard broom with stiff bristles.

The setting on the top right secured a large piece of board to the wall outside and attached large pieces of paper to it. The setting on the bottom right used an old white sheet tacked onto a board.

It is often more practical to use large sheets of cardboard, flattened boxes or whole boxes to paint outdoors. Children of all ages particularly enjoy decorating large cardboard boxes and playing with them afterwards. Providing various types of paper, sticky tape and glue increases the range of skills that the children will develop. Once the box is dry it can be brought indoors for the children to play with or in.

Children do not always need paper to paint and make marks on, or brushes to make marks with. Activities for mark making outdoors include using sticks in mud to make shapes and patterns; painting on wet tarmac; using chalk to make patterns or draw pictures on the ground; painting walls and fences with big brushes and buckets of water; throwing tennis balls dipped in paint against an old sheet attached to a wall or fence; and even painting in the snow using powder paints!

Talking About Paintings

Key ideas

The very best way to talk with children about their painting, or any mark making, is to be there with them while they are doing it. For this to happen regularly, adults must plan to spend time in the painting area, to help children get organised and to talk with them while they are busy making marks. Sometimes it is helpful to ask other children to come and have a look at what a child is painting. This can inspire other children to do their own painting, to begin to talk with each other or join in painting together.

Possible conversations

Younger children need to give their full attention to what they are doing, so it is often best for adults to make short comments. Once the children have finished, you can talk to them in more detail about what they have done.

Helpful comments to get children talking might include: 'You've chosen the green paint. That's a big splodge.' 'Oh, now you've got some red paint. That's a nice long line. Whoops! You've put the red paintbrush in the white pot!' 'It looks like you painted a frog. Oh, it's Mummy, is it?'

Older children are often able to talk about what they are *going to do,* e.g. 'I'm gonna paint Daddy's car.' This opens up the chance for you to comment and ask a question, 'Oh, Daddy's car. I think he has a red one.' They also enjoy the comments that you make or your suggestions, e.g. 'What about the wheels? Shall we mix up some black paint so you can paint them?' Children can respond to comments and questions if they like, or may prefer to concentrate on their painting. Once children have finished, you can have detailed conversations with them about what they have done, possibly including other children, e.g. 'Look at Jayden's painting. It's his daddy's car. Let's see if Jayden would like to tell us all about his painting.'

Writing down what children say

Often we want to remember what children have said about their paintings. If you are going to write on the child's painting, please ask him first and show him what you are writing. Make sure that you use the type of handwriting agreed on in your setting (see page 26). Alternatively, write down what the child says on a sticky note and attach this to the back of the painting. If the painting is going on display, write what the child said and attach it as a caption.

Big Movements 1

Key ideas

Children need to be confident in their *gross-motor movements* and skills before they can learn to use smaller, *fine-motor* movements. This includes being able to sit and stand steadily. This will then allow them to concentrate on what they are doing with their hands. Children also need strength in their shoulders and arms. This allows them to use their arms and hands during an activity without getting tired, e.g. repeatedly stamping with a sponge on a big sheet of paper. Children can often make movements quickly and automatically but it becomes important to be able to move slowly, with control and accuracy.

Children need to know the names of as many body parts as possible and to be able to talk about movements. This allows them to talk about what they are doing, understand and give instructions, and talk about what they and other people are doing.

Activities

Throwing and catching games are fun and help children to develop the skills they need to use their arms and hands automatically. Singing and dance activities that involve big movements promote body awareness skills and children's language. Songs like *Heads, Shoulders, Knees and Toes,* and *Oh, We Can Play on the Big Bass Drum* are particularly useful for copying movements and developing language. *The Hokey Cokey* is great for developing a sense of left and right.

Sit with a small group of children in a circle. Make an action, e.g. jumping on the spot. Show the children how to copy your action when you chant, 'One, two, three… jump!' Go round the group asking each child to stand up and make a big action. Encourage the children to name the action, e.g. hopping. Other children then copy after chanting together, 'One, two, three… hop!' After everyone has had a go at making a movement, see if everyone can remember the movements and name them, e.g. 'Who can remember what Jamie did?' The next time you lead the group, challenge them to make two movements for others to copy, e.g. turn around *and* sit down.

Take photographs of children doing as many actions as possible as part of their everyday play, as well as posing for the camera. Show the children the photos and help them to name the actions. Make a display with the title, 'This is the way we can move outside.' Add captions for each photo, e.g. 'Brian can hop', 'Katie can climb on the ladder', etc. Once you have finished with the display, use the photos to make a photo book about movement to keep in your book area.

Big Movements 2

Key ideas

Young children are often most comfortable when they are squatting so will prefer to make marks on the ground or floor. Some very young children prefer to stand when they are making marks at a table. If you are planning to have four children at a table at a time, start by putting out only two chairs so children can choose whether to stand or sit. You can always get more chairs if children want them.

As children move around making large shapes and patterns, they actually get a physical sense of what it feels like to make shapes. This is essential for them to be able to make the same smaller shapes with their hands when writing.

Activities

One of the simplest and most exciting activities for all young children is to draw and write with chalks on the ground. Short, stubby chalks are best for all children because they don't break and last longer than thinner ones. Children love to collect stones. If you find that the stones can make a mark on the ground, show the children how to draw and write with them. This is often more fun than using chalks!

Children like to paint on the ground, e.g. on paving slabs. They can use small buckets with watery paint and thick brushes and rollers to paint over a large area. Smaller, thicker brushes will allow children to make patterns, shapes and pictures. Wearing rubber boots and allowing children to walk in a tray of paint and then stamp around, encourages them to make big movements and to talk about the big marks they have made. If you have a builder's tray full of water, children can have fun walking around until the paint has been washed off their wellies.

Natural materials

Show children how to make marks outdoors by using sticks in mud; their fingers in the sand; and stones, leaves, conkers, grass, straw and pine cones to make shapes, letters and write their name. Pieces of willow can be bent and tied together to make large shapes.

Items found outside

Make a collection of odds and ends that you might have outdoors or that you bring to the setting. These could include bricks, wood offcuts, string, rope, pieces of metal and plastic piping. Encourage the children to make big shapes with these, e.g. a face, spirals, circles and squares.

Take photos whenever you can and talk to the children about what they are doing as you take the images. Make books and displays of the photos so that the children talk regularly about what they enjoyed doing.

Moving to Music

Key ideas

Children respond naturally to music by moving. If you are in a large room with a group of children, or outside, play a piece of fast music and ask them to move around. They will automatically move quickly. Follow this with a slow piece and they will move slowly. Moving to music increases children's awareness of how to move and how to talk about movements. We can use music and movement activities to introduce shapes and patterns that children will eventually need for writing, including circles, straight lines and waves. Programmes such as *Write Dance* that involve music, singing, movement and mark making are very helpful enjoyable *(Write Dance in the Early Years: A Pre-Writing Programme for Children 3 to 5* by Ragnhild Oussoren – Lucky Duck Books).

Activities

In a large room or outside space, use masking tape, chalk or paint to make large shapes on the ground. Choose a different shape for each session, perhaps starting with long straight lines. Ask the children to sit in a row at the end of the line and play some quiet music. Show the children how to walk carefully and quietly along the line, one at a time, and then sit in a new row at the end of the line. In following weeks make circles, squares, zig zags and waves. If you are able, leave the lines on the floor or outside on the ground so children can push small cars or trains along the lines.

Teach children the song *London Bridge is Falling Down*. Draw a line leading to a big shape on the floor, e.g. a circle. Two children make a bridge by facing each other on either side of the circle, reaching their arms out and holding hands. The other children take turns to walk along the line and under the bridge. Once the children understand what to do, you can choose more pairs to make more bridges.

Play a piece of recorded music and explore with the children different ways of moving to the music. This could include walk, crawl, wiggle, etc. You will probably want to introduce a few different movements in each session. One way to inspire children to move in different ways is to look at story books and information books about animals. Talk about how the animals move, e.g. ducks waddle, snakes slither, puppies scamper, kangaroos hop with two feet together, etc. *Toddle Waddle* by Julia Donaldson and Nick Sharratt (Macmillan Books) is a great book to help children explore movements and sounds.

Suggested vocabulary

Walk; crawl; tiptoe; bounce; twirl; hop; creep; roll; jog; gallop; leap; skip; stomp; scamper; shuffle; zoom; grow; slither; fly; waddle; prance; plod; amble; swagger; stroll; zig zag; wiggle; stretch; reach

With thanks to Frances Turnbull, Independent Music Educator, Musicaliti, www.musicaliti.co.uk

Following Directions, Giving Directions

Key ideas

Writing involves making movements in certain directions. To write a letter correctly you need to know where to start and in what direction to move the pen. You need to know when to stop, when to go back and then what direction to move the pen to make the next part of the shape. This is known as *letter orientation.* You learn that letters make up words and that words in English are written on a page from left to right. Before children begin to make shapes that look like letters or actually form letters, they need to know how to move their bodies in all directions and to follow and give instructions. Then they can do the same with their arms, hands and fingers.

Activities

One of the best ways to develop a sense of moving in different directions, and talking about them, is to play with children in a playground. Pushing a child on a swing introduces the feeling for *forwards* and *backwards* and on a roundabout they can go *round and round.* Children can also tell you when to *stop, start again* and *go the other way.* On a seesaw they can go *up* and *down.*

Playing football involves running and kicking a ball in different directions.

You can set up an obstacle course for children to climb under and over, crawl through, or walk around.

On bikes and in cars children can move in all directions and particularly learn how to go *backwards* and *forwards.*

Books to encourage talk about directions

- *Bears in the Night* by Stan and Jan Berenstain (HarperCollins Children's Books)
- *Rosie's Walk* by Pat Hutchins (Little Simon)
- *We're Going on a Bear Hunt* by Michael Rosen and Helen Oxenbury (Walker Books Ltd)

You can use these and similar books to inspire children to make props for an obstacle course and set it up outdoors. Children can wear costumes and act out the story with an adult. Use photos of the children to make your own *Rosie's Walk* or *We're Going on a Bear Hunt* photo books.

Suggested vocabulary

Here; there; up; down; point; inside; outside; through; along; next to; beside; in; on; under; around; over; in front; behind; backwards; forwards; front; back; narrow; wide

Eye Movements 1

Key ideas

To be able to read we need to be able to control our eye movements. This includes moving our eyes so that we can look in one direction and then go back to the start again. This is known as *visual scanning*. To read English we need to be able to visually scan in a left-to-right direction, and then go back to the left again. Some languages are written from right to left, e.g. Hebrew, Arabic and Urdu. Chinese and Japanese are written vertically from top to bottom. When working with children learning English as an additional language, it will be important to know how their home language is written because they may need extra support with visual-scanning activities.

Very young children move their heads when they are visually scanning, but gradually begin to move their eyes only. It is helpful to introduce large visual-scanning activities with younger children and introduce other, smaller activities once they progress in fine-motor skills.

Activities

Lining-up objects

Children can be helped to line up various objects from left to right on a table or the ground, including small plastic animals, pieces of play dough, toy cars, coins, buttons, jam jar lids and pieces of construction equipment, such as Lego® and Duplo®. Outdoors you can use sticks, leaves, conkers and stones to make patterns from left to right and to see how long children can make the line.

Use a wooden train set to make a very long track and encourage the children to push the trains from left to right.

Horizontal displays

Stick a large sheet of lining paper on the ground. Wearing wellington boots, children can walk in paint and then walk along the length of the paper in a straight line. Later do the same with painty hand prints, and spots and dabs with a paintbrush. Display the sheets horizontally on the wall.

You can use this paper as backing paper for a display that encourages looking from left to right. Display large photos of the children's faces at the children's eye level along the length of a wall. Ask children to walk along the display, starting at the left, to see how many children they can name. Sit the children about three metres away from the display. Ask a child to stand up and point to each photo in turn, from left to right, while the rest of the group name them. While doing this, the children will be using head and eye movements as they scan.

Eye Movements 2

Activities

Weaving

Weaving is valuable to help strengthen hands, develop pincer grasp and hand-eye coordination, as well as teaching left, right and visual scanning. If your setting is surrounded by a fence with palisades or mesh, you can make it attractive by helping the children weave long strips of coloured cloth or coloured strong foil (often available from your local scrap bank). Alternatively, you can buy sections of plastic mesh fencing from your local DIY store and weave indoors to make a lively display (this looks particularly exciting if you add fairy lights).

Children can weave on a smaller scale with a frame made from sticks and string or wool. Use strips of coloured cloth to weave in and out. You can also make a card background with slits cut in it and weave coloured strips of card through the slots. As you and the children are weaving together, talk about the directions they are going in, including words and phrases such as: *in and out; start here on the left; stop there on the right; now go back.*

Using rollers

Use various sizes of decorating rollers in paint to roll lines on large sheets of paper, from left to right. Using these large objects and big movements helps the children understand about direction as their bodies get a sense for moving from left to right. Using small rollers on smaller pieces of paper helps children use the scanning movements that they will need for reading and writing.

Threading beads and blocks

Using large, coloured, wooden beads help children thread them on to a string, very thin dowelling rod, or a kebab stick with the pointed ends cut off. Children will usually hold the string up vertically as they are threading. To help them scan from left to right, place an empty piece of string or rod on a table and help them to thread blocks from left to right. Can they copy a pattern you have made?

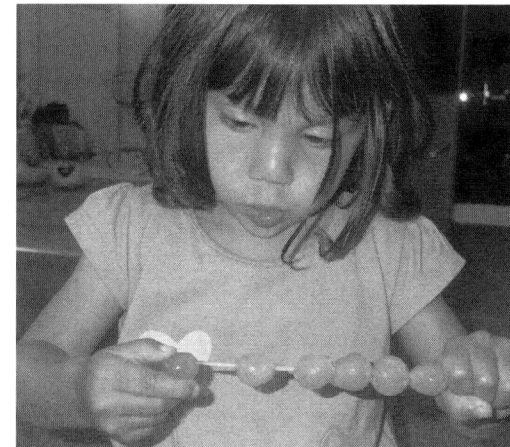

Fruit kebabs

Cut up pieces of fruit with the children and help them thread the pieces onto a kebab stick. Make a line with the fruit on the table first, beginning at the left. Put the kebab stick on the table next to the fruit so that the children can make a pattern from left to right. Make 'caterpillars' in the same way, using grapes.

Suggested vocabulary

Hands; fingers; body; left; right; line; that way (direction); forwards; towards; away from; along; weave; in; out; next; the next one; after that one; the last one; back

Thinking and Talking About Our Hands 1

Key ideas

As part of developing the skills involved in writing, children need to get to know their hands. This includes finding out what they can do with them and talking about what they can do. Our hands are very sensitive so there are many activities we can involve children in that raise their awareness of what they can feel with their hands. The aim of these fine-motor activities is that eventually children will be able to pick up and hold small objects, make slow controlled movements in a precise way, and eventually be able to do these things without thinking. This takes several years to learn!

Activities

Finger rhymes and songs are some of the best ways to introduce children to their hands and to help them remember the names for the various parts. *Wind the Bobbin Up, One Finger, One Thumb, Keep Moving, Two Little Dickie Birds* and *Tommy Thumb, Tommy Thumb Where Are You?* are all popular songs and rhymes. There are many finger rhymes and songs that involve counting with fingers. When teaching these songs and rhymes, it is very helpful to teach the words slowly at first, so that the children can learn to combine the words and actions.

Finger painting is perfect for developing children's awareness of how their hands feel (see page 8). You can also show children how to make shapes and patterns in sand with their index finger. You can do this in the sand tray as part of children's spontaneous play, or as an adult-led activity at a table using sand in a tray. Gradually adding small amounts of water to the sand changes what children can do with it. When sand becomes moist it is firm, so children can pinch it together between their thumbs and fingers to make shapes and patterns.

Using play dough to make rings with the children is another great way for children to learn to use their hands in different ways. Clay modelling also gives children a huge amount of stimulation as it is often cold, can be sticky or very firm, and you need to use a lot of strength and skill to make shapes and objects like pots. It requires a lot of adult supervision before, during and after the activity, so there will be lots for children to talk about with the adults and between themselves.

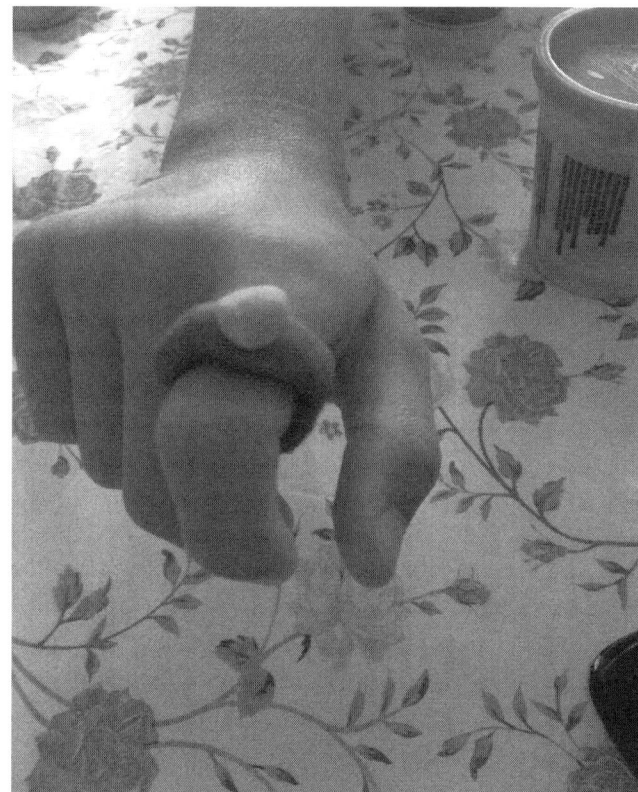

Thinking and Talking About Our Hands 2

Activities

Help children to draw round their hands and then encourage them to draw and colour in fingernails, a watch, rings and bracelets. Older children can draw round their hands and draw patterns. Make a wall display of all the hands.

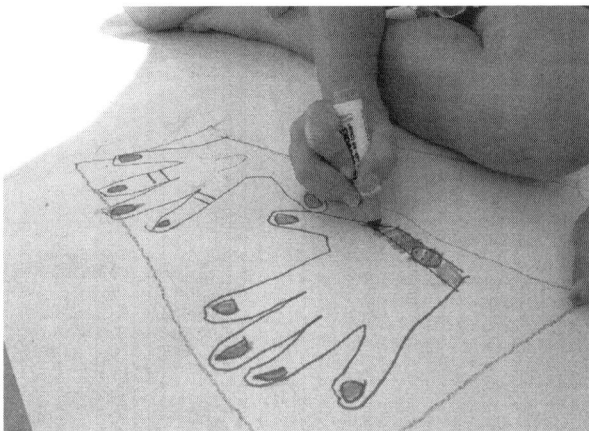

Putting on gloves is something children do every day in the winter. Children usually need adults to help them get their fingers in the right places, so this is an ideal chance to talk about children's fingers.

Make a wall display with the caption 'What can we do with our hands?' Take photos of children pointing, poking play dough, beckoning, squeezing, holding, picking up, sucking their thumb, stroking, holding on tight, letting go, scratching, drawing, writing, painting, etc.

Feeling activities

Use a feely box or feely bag to explore what children can feel with their hands. With younger children begin by putting one object in the bag, e.g. a ball, and seeing if the children can guess what it is.

Gradually introduce more objects that you know children will easily recognise, e.g. a wooden block, a piece of Duplo®. Can they feel three different objects and name them? With older children go on to introduce some items that are not so easy to recognise by feel, e.g. a key, a sock, a small teddy bear or small plastic animals.

When you are involved in everyday activities using your hands, talk to children about what you can feel with your hands, e.g. 'That water feels very hot. I'm going to add some cold water to make it warm. I'm going to dip my finger in very carefully to check how it feels.' Or, 'Look at these plants. They are very prickly.' Or, 'This glue is so sticky! It has stuck my fingers together!' This will encourage children to talk about their own hands.

In the same way, you can talk about how your hands feel, e.g. 'It's so cold today. Feel my hands. They are freezing! I'm going to put my gloves on.' Or, 'My hands are so hot, they have become all sweaty!'

Can you recognise your own hands?

Take a photo of each child's and adult's hands. Some children may want to add rings, bracelets and bangles to decorate their hands and fingernails. This will make their photo easier to identify. Make a wall display and then use the photos to make an 'Our Hands' book.

Suggested vocabulary

Fingers; nails; knuckles; wrist; thumb ('Tommy Thumb'); index finger/forefinger ('Peter Pointer'); middle finger ('Toby Tall'); ring finger ('Ruby Ring'); little finger/pinkie ('Baby Small'); palm of your hand; back of your hand; fist; bang; thump; squeeze; scratch; tap

Hand and Finger Control 1

Key ideas

Hand and finger control, or *manual dexterity*, develops as children become older and more experienced. Eventually they will be able to move each finger on its own and develop other skills, such as being able to place each finger and thumb together on one hand. This allows them to pick up very small objects between their fingers and thumb, and then to learn to comfortably hold a pen (see page 22 *Pencil Grasp*).

Hand control involves thinking about what you are going to do and then carefully doing it. For example, lining up cars on the edge of a table so that they don't fall off; placing a train on a wooden track so that the wheels fit on and then pushing the train along so it does not crash; and lining up dominoes and carefully knocking the first one over so that they all fall down.

Children begin by grasping objects in the palm of their hand *(palmar grasp)* and work towards being able to pick up a small object between their thumb and index finger *(pincer grasp)*. When they first develop these movements and skills, they need to look at what they are doing as part of the growth of hand-eye coordination. With repeated practice they can make many movements without looking, or even with their eyes closed!

Activities

There are many activities that we offer children in early years settings that develop hand and finger control, including threading beads, making models with construction toys, building with small wooden blocks, cutting with scissors, completing puzzles and using play dough.

There are also fun activities that you can introduce to children with the specific purpose of developing their hand control. Activities with an element of competition are often particularly popular, e.g. 'Let's see if we can squeeze these sponges until they are dry. Let's see if we can fill this bucket up with water squeezed from these sponges.' Here the children are not competing against each other but testing their own strength.

Using tongs and tweezers, see how many pompoms you can move from a container into muffin cases on a baking tray. You could set children a target of putting three pompoms in each case. Younger children will enjoy this activity if they are allowed to use just their fingers!

Hand and Finger Control 2

Activities

Encourage children to pick up small coins and post them into a money box. This will develop children's pincer grasp – as well as encouraging counting!

Turn a colander upside down and help children push coloured pipe cleaners through the holes. Children get very excited about filling all the holes and the end result can make a very attractive hat! *Whatever Next?* by Jill Murphy (Macmillan Children's Books) has an illustration of a teddy bear with a colander on his head. Sharing the book with the children is a great way to stimulate them to get involved in this activity.

Flick football

This is a game for two children at a time. For the activity you need a light pompom or a table tennis ball and a table. Help children to draw a football pitch on a large sheet of paper. Make a goal at each end by using masking tape to stick straws or pieces of paper rolled into small tubes together. Show the children how to flick the ball with their thumb and index finger and see who can score the most goals!

Making pictures out of pre-cut shapes

Help children to make pictures or patterns out of a selection of coloured shapes. Using different types of glue will develop different types of hand control. Using a chunky glue stick will be ideal for younger children who can grip it in their fist *(palmar grasp)*. Smaller, thinner glue sticks encourage children to hold the stick between thumb, middle finger and ring finger. Using a glue stick with PVA glue encourages the same movement.

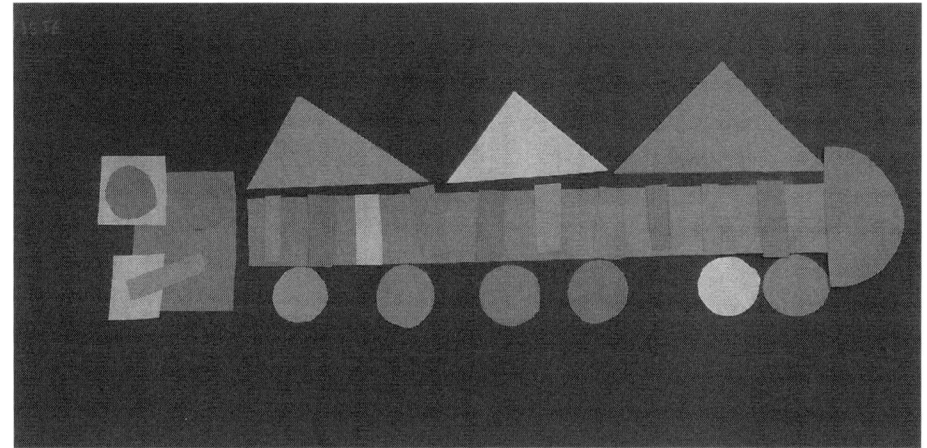

Suggested vocabulary

Pick up; between your fingers; thumbs; careful; gentle; flick; post; push; pull; hold; squeeze; let go/release; cut; paste; glue; stick

Making Our Hands Strong

Key ideas

Children need to have strong hands in order to grip objects such as pens and chalks and to sometimes press firmly for quite a long time. Drawing and colouring with chalks on the ground or with wax crayons on a large sheet of paper, for example, requires quite a lot of strength. Strengthening children's grip involves most of the muscles of the hands and arms. An important part of being strong is knowing when to apply a lot of force and when to be gentle.

Activities

Use cloths in warm soapy water to wash windows, cars, bikes and scooters. Encourage children to squeeze the cloths as hard as they can to get all the dirty water out. Help the children rinse out the cloths to make sure that they are clean and all the soap has gone. Encourage the children to squeeze the cloths to make them as dry as they can and then peg them on the line to dry. Put sponges, flannels, shower puffs and some baby dolls in the water tray. Encourage the children to squeeze the sponges and puffs as they wash the babies.

Allow children to squeeze ready-mixed paint out of the bottle before and during painting activities. Put empty ready-mixed paint bottles in the water tray. This activity is particularly popular if there is some paint left in the bottom!

Make play dough with the children, ensuring it is particularly firm so that children have to work hard to knead the dough, make it smooth and make shapes.

Rope swings or pulling hard on a rope; e.g. as part of a climbing frame, strengthens grip, arms and shoulders.

Using Paper

Tearing paper particularly develops fine-motor coordination. Use torn paper strips to put in a large bucket to make a lucky dip. Add toys and see if the children can feel in the bucket and guess what the toys are.

Scrunching paper into a tight ball with two hands together develops arm and wrist strength. Using masking tape to wrap around the paper ball will make it surprisingly strong, as well as developing children's fine-motor skills. Make a target with the children and see if they can throw the balls and hit the target. Younger children can have a go at throwing as many balls as they can into a bucket or cardboard box. Make a big ball from paper and use it for children to catch by bringing two hands together.

It is best to use different types of recycled paper for these activities and recycle the paper with the children once you have finished.

Cooking

This involves many activities that develop children's hand strength as well as their manual dexterity. These include chopping vegetables or cheese, spreading, stirring cake mixture, kneading dough, or rubbing flour, milk and butter together to make scones. Cooking also stimulates a huge amount of conversation!

Suggested vocabulary

Squeeze; scrunch; tear; rip; fold; cut; pull; push; climb; throw; catch; wet; dry; damp

Pencil Grasp

Key ideas

Young children begin by holding mark-making tools in the palm of their hand. This is fine for random repeated movements *(scribbling)*, but less useful for more sophisticated marks. As children grow they begin to use a *pincer grasp*, gripping the pen between their thumb and forefinger, or, in many cases, between the thumb and a combination of all their fingers. Once children have a pincer grasp, they can learn to hold a pencil with a *tripod grasp*. This is the way that most children in the UK hold a pen for writing.

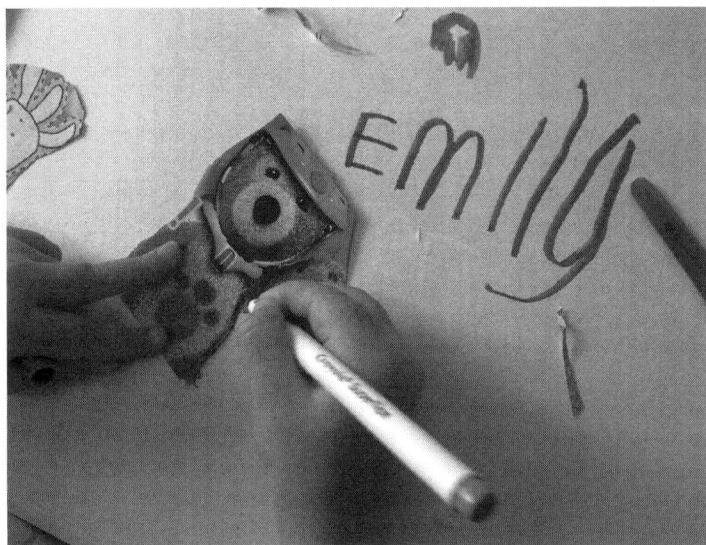

We aim for children to hold a pen in a way that is comfortable and allows them to make accurate movements without grasping the pen too tightly or pressing too hard. You can test whether your colleagues are holding a pen in a relaxed way by gently pulling the pen out of their grasp while they are writing. If the pen comes away from their grasp easily, then you know that they were holding it in a relaxed way!

Most children learn the tripod grasp, but if you take a look at the way adults write you will find that there are many variations. Handwriting specialists say that it is best to encourage children to use a mature tripod grasp early on, as it sometimes can be difficult to teach children to change their grasp if they have grown up holding a pen in a particular way. It is the adults' job to judge whether or not we should focus on how a child holds a pen, or concentrate more on building his confidence in mark making and early writing. In some cases it might be better to wait until children are comfortable with writing all their letters before focusing on teaching them how to use a tripod grasp. It will be important to discuss this with parents so that everyone is clear about which approach they all intend to take in the setting and at home.

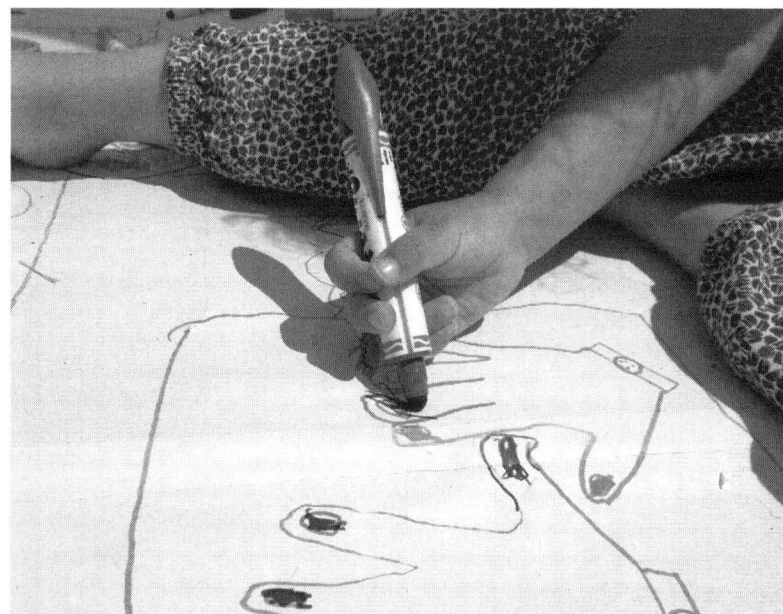

Being Right- or Left-Handed or Both!

Key ideas

We describe people as being either right- or left-handed, depending on which hand they prefer to use for fine-motor activities such as writing, holding a spoon or using tools. We talk about *laterality* to describe the preference that most people have for using an arm, leg, foot and eye from one side of the body. For most people their brain has gradually 'decided' which hand, foot and eye they will use automatically or prefer to use. As a result, we build up strength on one side of the body more than the other.

Try this on yourself using a ball and a small cardboard tube. Kick the ball and then throw it. Which foot and hand did you use? Now look through the cardboard tube and look at the ball. Which hand did you use to pick up the tube with and which eye did you hold it up to? If your answer was 'my right' for each of these questions then we can say that you are 'right dominant', because you prefer to use your right side. If your answer was 'left' then you are 'left dominant'.

Laterality and 'handedness' develop through early experiences of moving and touching: using the whole body as well as different limbs. Some children as early as eight months of age show a preference for using one hand more than another, e.g. always picking up a spoon with the left hand. For others, their handedness is not decided until around three years of age. Up to that point they might pick up a crayon with one hand, begin drawing with the other and while they are drawing pass the crayon between both hands.

When problems arise

Some older children have mixed laterality, where their brains have not yet decided whether they will be right- or left-handed. This *may* be a sign that the child could have additional learning needs, e.g. *dyslexia.* However, some children take longer to develop a preference or may even become ambidextrous where they can use both hands equally well (though this is quite rare). All children benefit from activities to develop movement and children with undecided or mixed laterality benefit from extra support with large and small movements. When assessing children with additional learning needs, professionals always look closely at laterality and handedness. Occupational therapists and physiotherapists in particular are able to carry out in-depth assessments and give practical advice on how to help children develop their laterality.

Supporting left-handed children

Children who are left-handed can use the same mark-making tools as other children, though left-handers need to use scissors designed specifically for their needs. These scissors are often difficult for right-handers to use. It is very important that your setting has several pairs of left-handed scissors (their handles are usually a different colour to those used by right-handers).

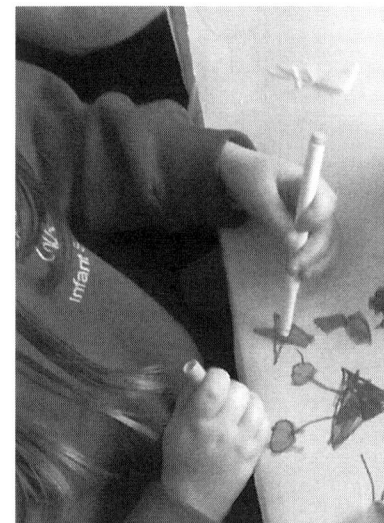

Shapes, Mark Making and Early Writing

Key ideas

To be able to write in English, children need to be able to know about and draw circles, squares, horizontal lines, vertical lines and lines at an angle. If we add dots to our list of shapes, then children eventually will be able to make most of the letter shapes needed for printing (see page 26).

Before children can draw shapes they need to be able to recognise them and know what they are called. There are many books and games that adults can share with children to help. To be able to draw a shape, children need to be able to make shapes in the air with their arms, hands and fingers, make shapes with play dough, with sticks on the ground or in the sand. Moving along very large shapes outside gives children an understanding of how different shapes are made.

Activities

Everything in nature, everything we build or put inside our buildings is made up of shapes. Introduce the children to a different shape each week and take the children looking indoors and outdoors for those shapes. Take photos and collect as many objects as you can, and display them on a shapes table or wall display. For example, circles can be found in flowers, hoops, the bottom of a bucket and even a slice of cucumber!

Outdoors, use chalk or paint to draw a very long line. Ask children to get on bikes or in toy cars and pull/push them along the line, go to the end of the line and then turn round and go back. They can go one at a time or follow closely after each other – children love to make traffic jams! Draw more lines until you have made a square. Encourage children to push and pull each other around the shape. You can repeat the activity with a new shape each day.

Put paint on the wheels of bikes/trikes and let the children drive through puddles in clockwise and anti-clockwise directions.

On large sheets of paper or on the ground, draw around hula hoops with chalk. Talk about the shape as children are drawing. To help children understand curves, draw round one half of the hoop with one colour and then the remaining half with another colour. Introduce the word *curve* as you are doing it.

Dip the wheels of small toy cars in paint and encourage the children to draw different shapes using the toys. For example, driving a car round the outline of a paving slab might make an excellent square.

Suggested vocabulary

Shapes; along; across; up; down; straight; round; curve; curved; half; forwards; back; backwards; around; inside; outside; in front of; behind

Patterns

Key ideas

A pattern is a series of repeated shapes or movements. In nature, movements can make patterns, e.g. when we throw a stone in a pond we make ripples in a series of circles, or when we splash in the bath we can make a pattern of waves. Buildings and other man-made objects also have patterns, including a series of solid shapes, e.g. a wall made of bricks or six rectangular panes of glass in a window frame.

Children need to make and understand patterns with objects before they can learn to draw them and eventually use them in writing. In pre-writing and writing, we encourage children to look for and make patterns that are continuous – where there is no break in a line; e.g. zig zags, waves or spirals – where the tip of the pen stays on the page. This is particularly important for understanding joined-up writing and for recognising some letters such as m and w.

Activities

Use small cars to make a traffic jam: red car, blue car, red car, blue car, etc. Alternatively use beads threaded on a lace.

Make repeating patterns using coloured wooden blocks or flat plastic shapes and then gummed shapes. Patterns can be very simple, such as red block, blue block, red block, blue block, and lead to more complex patterns, e.g. using more colours and shapes.

When children are painting, comment on the patterns they are making, e.g. 'I can see a wavy pattern there. Are you going to make another one?' Or, 'That looks like a spiral. Is it a snail?'

Many children's books have vivid illustrations or photos that can inspire children to recognise and draw patterns. Here is a short list:

- *Snail Trail* by Ruth Browne (Andersen Press): spirals and other shapes
- *Little Boat* by Thomas Docherty (Templar Publishing): circles, spirals and waves
- *Hooray for Fish!* by Lucy Cousins (Walker Books Ltd). Her bright and exciting designs can be used to talk about patterns and to inspire children to make their own patterns
- *Peck Peck Peck* by Lucy Cousins (Walker Books Ltd). Another bright and bold book that particularly helps children understand and make dots and spots
- non-fiction books about sharks: for points and zig zags.

Suggested vocabulary

Pattern; again; repeat; same; round; wave/s; wavy; point; up; down; zig zag; line; straight; curve

Handwriting Styles

Key ideas

There is a big debate about how best to teach children to write. Should we teach *printing* (writing letters separately in words without joining them up) or *continuous cursive* or *cursive script,* (where letters are joined together in words)? Some experts feel that once children have learned to print, it can be very difficult for them to learn to write cursively. In France, for example, all children are taught to write using continuous cursive script when they first start writing. (French teachers also spend a lot of time helping children to experiment with shapes and patterns because this helps children develop the skills needed for joined-up writing.) Other experts suggest it doesn't matter how you write, as long as children see examples of continuous cursive script and printing, e.g. in books, when adults write and in the displays on the walls. Many children say they find it easier to read print. To prove this point, very few children's books are actually written in a continuous cursive script.

If you decide to use printing in your setting, choose a style *(font)* that has 'flicks'. These are short curls at the bottom of the letters **a, d, h, i, k, l, m, n, t** and **u.** This helps children link their letters more easily when they begin to learn to write with a continuous cursive script when they are older.

You will also need to decide how adults are going to write numbers with children because in the UK there are variations in the style used. Parents from other countries might have a different style for writing numbers too.

Adults' handwriting

When working with young children, *how* adults write is just as important as *what* they write. When we write with children, we hope that they will watch us carefully and copy our *handwriting.* And many of them do! Some children watch everything we do:

- the way that we hold a pen
- the way we form our letters, including what direction we form letters *(letter orientation)* such as **a** and **o**
- whether we use *continuous cursive script* or *printing*
- whether we write with capitals *(upper case)* or small letters *(lower case).*

What we write in children's observation folders, home-school books and on children's work should be neat and easy to read. When we write captions for wall displays, this should be in the style or *script* that everyone in the setting has agreed to use. This also applies to captions that have been printed from the computer. In this way, children and parents will see that there is a particular standard that you set for handwriting, and parents and children can copy this.

Important point: If your setting is part of a school, then you should follow your school's handwriting policy. If there is a school near your setting where most of the children move to, you might find it useful to discuss handwriting with the reception teachers, so your styles are similar.

Letters and Sounds: Principles and Practice of High Frequency Phonics (DFES, 2007) has a useful letter formation chart in Appendix 2.

Role-Play Writing

Key ideas

Children imitate what adults and older children do. As children play they often use what they have seen adults do and say. This is an important part of their learning as they try to make sense of things that they have seen or heard. This is also true for mark making and early writing where we often see children pretending to write *(role-play writing)*. Role-play writing is very important because it helps children understand that writing is useful as part of everyday life. Children who write a lot as part of role play also gain practice in the skills they need for writing. Sometimes children write naturally as part of their play, e.g. writing a shopping list on a scrap of paper while they are pretending to go to the shops. We need to provide mark-making resources in areas where children are role playing to encourage them to write as part of their play, e.g. attaching a whiteboard to the wall with a marker pen on a piece of string in the home corner so children can use it for shopping lists.

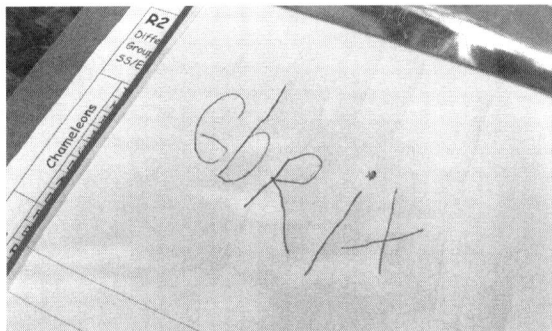

'6 bricks' was written by a child pretending to be behind the counter at a builders' yard. We can see that he knows about some letter sounds and how to write corresponding letters. He understands the difference between letters and numbers too. At this stage it is not important that he is using upper- and lower-case letters.

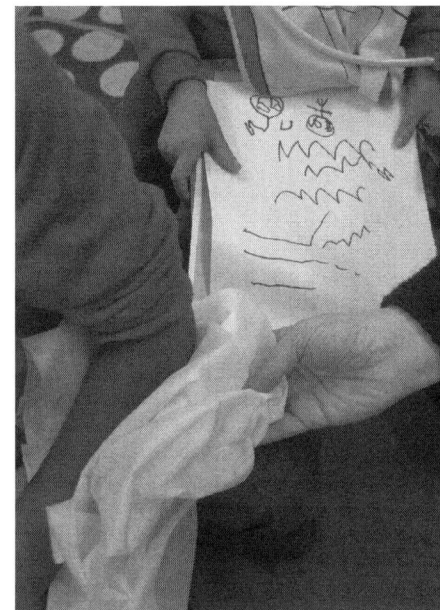

As part of playing in the hospital, this doctor has written, 'Carl has broken his arm. We need to cut it off'! We can see that he knows that adults write in lines and that their 'joined-up' writing can look like a zig zag.

Important point: When children are involved in role-play writing, it is important to pretend that you understand what they have written rather than looking at how they have formed their letters and numbers. If you start to talk about their actual writing, e.g. praising them for the way they have formed their letters, this stops becoming play and becomes a lesson. This will stop the children from focusing on their imaginative play.

Role-Play Areas for Mark Making

Key ideas and activities

It can be useful to set up particular role-play areas that will naturally involve a lot of writing, e.g. a Post Office, doctors' surgery or even a school office! These work best when adults and children create the area together. Most importantly, adults need to get involved in the play to show how adults use writing as part of everyday life. Children love this and it often gives them exactly the inspiration they need to pretend to be writers.

Suggested role-play areas

A garage – where mechanics examine cars and write on clipboards what is wrong with the cars.

A bank – where there are many slips of paper on a counter and pens attached to little chains or strings. Children write on the slips, put them in envelopes and post them in a 'Credit point'.

A Post Office – where children weigh and send parcels, buy stamps, get money and post items in a letterbox outside.

A parking meter outdoors – where children take turns to be the driver, or the traffic warden who writes in a notepad and sticks the 'fine notice' on the car windscreen.

A shoe shop – where children measure each other's feet and write down what size they are.

A building site – where children measure with tape measures how long pieces of scrap wood are and write numbers with pencils on the wood.

A hospital – where all of the patients have a chart on a clipboard at the end of the bed for doctors and nurses to write notes.

A café – where the waiter writes down the customers' orders on a small pad of paper and shows this to the chef.

A launderette and dry cleaners – where customers leave their washing in bags and are given a ticket with the date, name of the items and price on. You can also have children's magazines for them to colour in and write on while they are waiting for their washing to finish its cycle in the machines.

A builders' yard – where the staff behind a counter write down on clipboards what the customer wants and deliver it to the customer's car or home.

Argos – a fascinating shop where customers look in catalogues and write down on a small piece of paper what they want, and pass it to a member of staff behind the counter who gets the item from a warehouse behind the counter.

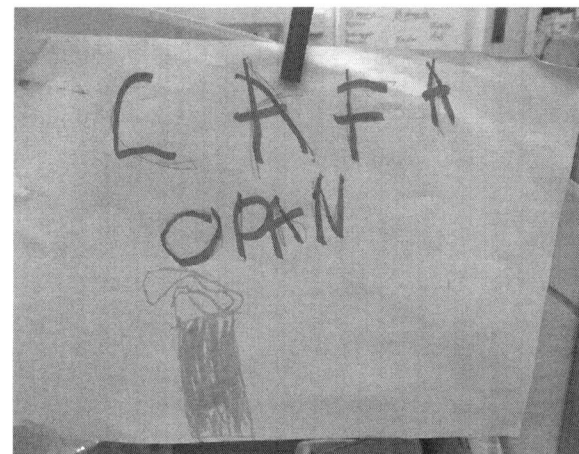

This child made a sign for their café role-play area. The adults were delighted and pegged the sign up temporarily above the café door. On another day they talked with the child about how the words 'café' and 'open' are actually written, and made another sign for her to put up permanently.

Developmental (Emergent) Writing 1

Key ideas

As children grow and become more experienced with mark making they begin to experiment with writing letters. They do this as part of their play and particularly if they see adults around them writing, as part of their work or everyday life at home. Children often imitate what they see older brothers and sisters writing, including writing for homework. Children often pretend to write in registers that they have made as they imitate what staff in early years settings do at registration.

When we look at what the children have written, we begin to see them make shapes and patterns, or patterns that start to look like writing. This might be a series of lines and dots or waves and zig zags that represent joined-up writing. At first these might be part of a child's drawing, but gradually the child does his 'writing' separately from what he has drawn. This shows us that he is beginning to understand the difference between drawing and writing. This phase in children's early writing is known as *developmental* or *emergent writing* because it develops or emerges naturally as children's knowledge about and experience of reading and writing increases.

Later we begin to see strings of letters and shapes that look like letters. Some of these often come from the child's name. Children also draw symbols, such as hearts and kisses.

Gradually, we begin to see the child fill whole sheets with letters. Sometimes we can see that they have tried to copy words that they have seen on wall displays, in magazines or books in or near the mark-making area. Sometimes children write letters that are back-to-front, but these *reversals* are often part of a stage that children go through. This shows us that they have not fully understood that letters need to have a particular *orientation* and be written in English from left to right.

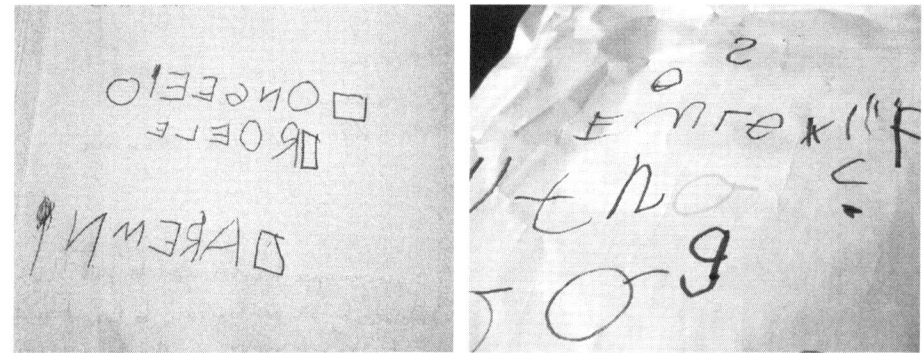

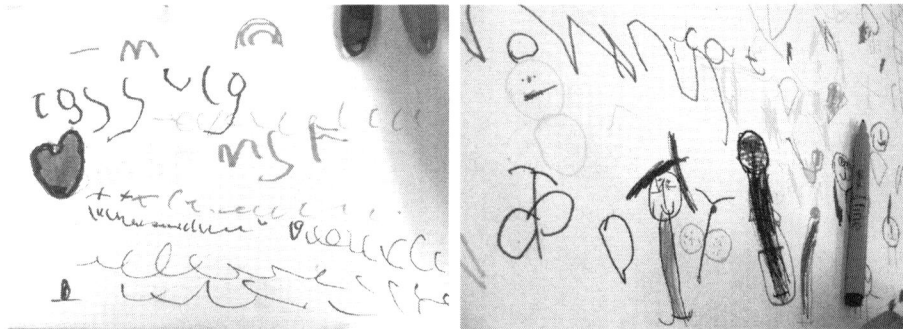

Developmental (Emergent) Writing 2

Key ideas

Developmental writing is a very important stage in children's progress as early writers. By looking closely at what they have written spontaneously, we can see what children understand about writing and reading. For example, a child who writes long strings of letters might not yet know that letters are grouped together to make words. On the other hand, a child who regularly writes letters in groups might already have this knowledge.

This child wrote this caption to a photo of a fire station after a visit to a real fire station. We can see that she understands that each word we say should be written as an individual word. She writes mainly using capital letters but also some lower case. Her understanding of spelling is developing very well too!

The adults' role

Adults who spend time with children while they are writing are in the best position to talk to them and support their learning. Children often show adults scraps of paper with developmental writing on and ask the adult, 'What does that say?' Or, 'Can you read this for me?' At times, adults will see something that a child has written and want to say something helpful which will develop the child's understanding. There are various ways to respond that children can find interesting, rewarding and sometimes very funny! These include:

- 'I love your writing!'
- 'What have you written about?'
- 'I can see lots of letters. Some of them are in your name.' (Wait for the child to say something and see where the conversation goes.)
- 'Shall I have a go at reading what you have written?' (Then try and pronounce some of the sounds together so they sound like words. This can make children laugh a lot.)
- 'Goodness! That looks like you have written 'dog'. It is dog? Shall I show you how to write it so it looks right?'

In all of these examples, the children know that what they have written is unlikely to be completely correct. Because they were playing when they wrote it, they will usually be happy for you to pretend to 'read' what they have written as if it is a message made up of correctly formed words.

Recognising My Name

Key ideas

Many parents see their child being able to write his name as an important milestone in their child's development. Many children are naturally keen to do this too. Part of their early writing often involves them either pretending to write their name or writing strings of shapes and letters that come from their name.

A child needs to be able to recognise his name before he can write it. This includes knowing that his name can be written and that his name can be seen in lots of different places, e.g. above his peg, on name tags in his clothes and on his paintings. The more a child sees adults writing his name, the sooner he will begin to recognise what his name looks like. For example, if every time before a child starts painting an adult takes time to write the child's name carefully on the paper and talk with the child about the letters, the child will soon learn to recognise his name and start to notice how the various letters are formed.

The more children are involved in activities which include recognising names and in conversations about names, the more likely they will be to take a spontaneous interest in writing their name.

Activities

Make a name card for each child with their name handwritten on strong card and laminated or covered in sticky-backed clear plastic. For very young children it helps to have a small photo of the child on the card too. Use the cards for registration. Place all the cards on a table. Parents can help children find their card and stick it on a chart or on a wall display with a caption that says, for example, 'Who is in nursery today?'

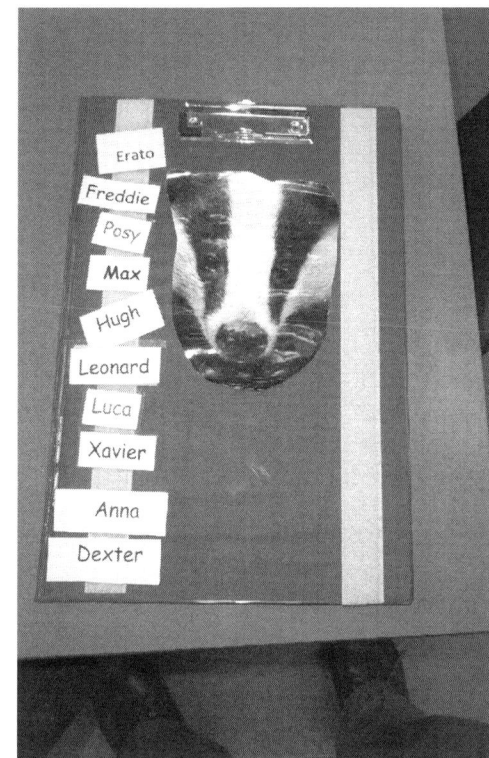

In this setting each family group has a clipboard with a photo of the animal their group is named after. Parents help children move their name from the Velcro strip on the left side of the clipboard to the right, to show that they are in nursery. There is also a piece of paper on the table so that children can have a go at writing their name too.

It can be a good idea to make stickers with the child's name on, so that they can take them to stick on their paintings, models, drawings, etc. for display and to take home.

Beginning to Write My Name

Key ideas

Children often begin to try to write their name spontaneously. This shows that they already have a lot of understanding about writing. In this early stage it is not important how they form the letters, what size they are, whether they are *capital letters* or *lower case* or a mixture of both, or whether the child wrote the letters in the right direction (*orientation*). What is important is that young children recognise their name and are happy to have a go at writing letters or pretending to write their name. Adults should praise the children's efforts. It can be helpful to say things like, 'You've had a go at writing your name! I can see the D for David. Mummy and daddy will be pleased when we show them at home time.'

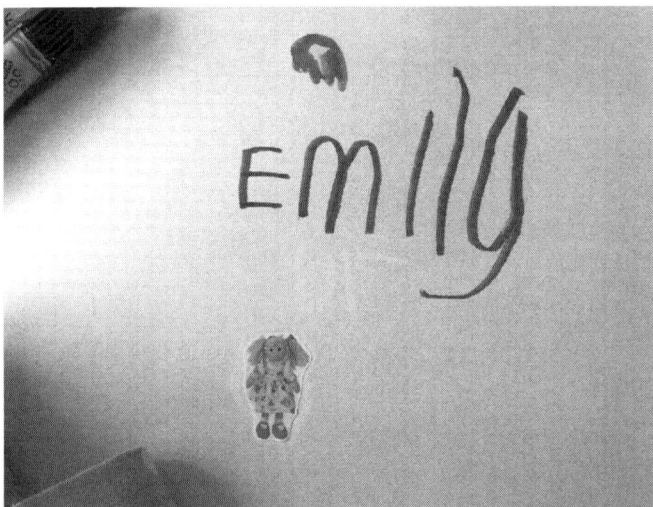

Emily wrote her name without being asked. She knows that the first letter of her name is 'a big letter' (i.e. a capital letter) and can say the letters of her name as she writes. How she forms the letters, or the size of each letter, is not important at this stage.

Many children take pleasure in writing their name and go through a phase of writing it everywhere they can, including in books, on walls and even on bedsheets! Parents are likely to be very pleased with their children's achievement too. Once a child writes their name confidently, you can discuss with parents the importance of praising the child without focusing on how letters are formed.

Activities

Children will be ready to focus on writing their name when they, like Emily in the photo to the left, do so spontaneously and even ask for help. One of the best ways to give help is to sit next to the child and show them how to write your own name. Use a yellow highlighter pen to write your own name, making sure you talk about each letter and give a commentary as you form it. For example, 'My name is Michael. It begins with a big letter M. I write it like this.' When you have written the letters, look at the child's name card and talk about any letters that are the same on his name card. Use a pencil to write your name again, going over the yellow letters of your highlighter pen.

If children show an interest in writing their own name, use the same technique but help them by writing their name first with the highlighter pen, and talk with them while they use a pencil to write within your yellow letters.

Important Point: When helping children to write, always sit to the right of the child. This allows you to see what the child is writing. Also, if you point at something he has written, he can see clearly what you are pointing at. When you are writing something for him, it helps if he sits on your right.

Talking About Numbers

Key ideas

We quite rightly think of early writing being mainly about letters and words, but understanding, recognising and beginning to write numbers is very important too. Children take an interest in numbers in the same way as they do with reading and writing – by talking about numbers as part of everyday activities, being involved in number activities and sharing books with numbers.

Many conversations with young children involve numbers, e.g. 'How old are you?' 'Show me three fingers. Yes, you will have three candles and a big number three on your cake.' 'How old are you going to be at your next birthday?' Children regularly sing songs about numbers, e.g. *Five Currant Buns, Ten Green Bottles, Ten in the Bed.*

There are two important ways we use numbers that children must learn before they can use numbers accurately:

- numbers follow a sequence, so children learn to count, 'One, two, three, four, five …'
- a number can stand for an amount, e.g. the word *three* and the symbol 3 mean that there are three things that we are talking about – three fingers, currant buns, spots on a dice, teddies in bed, bears, little pigs or Billy Goats Gruff.

Activities

Take the children for a number walk down the street. Talk about all the numbers they can see. These will include numbers on buses, road signs, shop signs and car registration plates. This helps children to notice numbers and to talk about how numbers can be used in different ways, and not just for counting.

Set up a number table with as many household appliances and everyday objects you can find with numbers on. This could include weighing scales, clocks, a watch and a mobile phone. Point out that the numbers on many digital displays look different to the way we write numbers. Encourage the children to choose an object to draw, including any numbers they can see. Make a display of their drawings, with a caption such as 'Numbers in our nursery'. Ask parents to talk with their children about numbers on the way home and at home. Ask them to make a list of all the items they can find with numbers on. Ask them to choose one object and make a drawing of it to display in the nursery.

Sing and play *What's the Time Mr. Wolf* to draw children's attention to numbers and clocks. Make a clock out of cardboard with the children to use when singing songs about time, e.g. *Hickory, Dickory Dock.*

Steve Grocott has produced an excellent set of CDs of number songs, available from: www.thesheetmusiccompany.co.uk

Writing Numbers

Key ideas

Just like learning to write letters, at first it is not important how children write numbers. The most important thing is that they know what numbers are for and have a go at writing them. When children begin to role-play writing, they often write strings of letters and numbers together. Gradually they begin to show that they understand that letters and numbers are different.

As with letter formation, all adults in the setting will need to agree how to write numbers with children and on displays. How adults write numbers varies across the world, so it will be useful to talk to parents about the way you have agreed to write numbers in your setting.

When teaching children how to write numbers accurately, it is helpful to point out their shapes, e.g. 'What do you think the number 2 looks like? A swan? Or maybe a duck?' 'I think number 8 looks like a snowman. Look. There are two circles, one on top of the other. Or is it like a fat teddy bear? What do you think it looks like?'

Writing 'very big numbers'

As part of a project based on *Jack and the Beanstalk,* children were shown how to measure themselves on a height chart. This led to a lot of talk about what the children called 'very big numbers'. The adults gave the children a long till roll from the local supermarket. One of the children was very proud that he could write numbers from 0 to 100. Other children were so impressed they wanted to copy him!

Suggested vocabulary

Number; next; altogether; forwards; backwards; shape; straight line; curve; how many?

Useful reading

Let's Talk About Maths! by Michael Jones and Judith Twani (Lawrence Educational)
Everyday Maths Through Everyday Provision by Elaine Bennett and Jenny Weidner (Routledge)

Construction Outdoors

Key ideas and activities

As with early writing, it is important that children see that adults write numbers for a good reason. One of the main reasons why adults write numbers outdoors is when they are measuring. This is usually during building and making repairs outside the home. People who are measuring and cutting wood, for example, use a tape measure and make marks on the wood before they cut. On building sites, you will often see numbers written on walls before they are painted (including telephone numbers!). This idea inspired children to get involved in making marks while involved in construction outdoors.

Show the children the lengths of wood. They are likely to want to dress up as builders immediately and make their own constructions. As they are playing show them how to measure with a tape measure and how to mark the wood where they might want to cut. Show them the number of centimetres and write the number on the piece of wood.

It is essential that the children are carefully supervised while using the tape measures. Hold the measure and explain how it is used, then children can handle the measures. If you decide to involve the children in hammering, sawing and screwing then they will need to be supervised very closely. Many settings regularly encourage their children to get involved in construction with real tools, so introducing mark-making and writing numbers on wood will be a natural extension of what they already do. Children usually get involved in drawing lines, writing numbers and talking about measuring. Sometimes girls may need to be encouraged to be involved by giving them a reason for playing, e.g. finding some minibeasts and making a home for them.

Resources needed

Small tape measures in a range of attractive colours; hard hats; children's high-visibility vests; stubby pencils; at least 30 offcuts of wood in various sizes (often can be donated). If the wood has splinters children can be supervised to sand these down. This is an excellent activity for strengthening hands.

Additional items: a saw; hammers; nails; screwdrivers; screws; children's-sized writing belts containing a pen, a pencil, a notepad and a mobile phone – children wear them around their waists, in the same way that builders wear tool belts (available from www.heritagetreasurebaskets.co.uk).

Suggested vocabulary

Write; draw; measure; line; cut; tape measure; careful; fit together; long; longer; longest; how long?; short; shorter; shortest; how short?

Useful reading

Playing and Learning Outdoors by Jan White (Routledge)

Using Small-World Animals

Key ideas and activities

Sometimes it can be very exciting for children to use different mark-making materials together. A popular activity involves groups of children using small-world animals, felt pens, play dough and natural materials such as sticks, stones and leaves to create a story.

Ask the children to help you cover the table with paper. The handling of pieces of masking tape and cutting paper is great for fine-motor skills and encourages a lot of interest and talk!

Around the table, share a story with the children about farm animals or African wild animals, depending on which set of animals you are using. Share out the animals. Introduce the felt pens and see how the

children respond. Some may immediately begin to draw food, a river, mud or even beds for their animals. Encourage children to look at what each other is doing. Gradually introduce the natural materials and see how the children respond. Often they will make homes and begin to make up stories with their animals, using the felt pens to draw. Finally, introduce the play dough. Soon you will have the paper full of exciting marks!

Children can get deeply involved with this activity, so plan for adults to be with the children for at least an hour. It works best when two adults are able to take part.

Resources needed

A roll of lining paper to cover a table; masking tape; thick and thin felt pens in containers; a basket of natural materials, including small sticks, pebbles, shells, lengths of wool and small pieces of fleece; play dough; a set of farm animals or African wild animals; books about animals

Using Magazines

Key ideas and activities

Children love magazines based on their favourite TV programmes and films. There are usually free stickers for the children to handle and talk about and activities that encourage mark making, such as join the dots, simple mazes and colouring in. The following activity is particularly successful in encouraging children to make marks who would not normally do so. It often lasts for at least an hour and works best if a minimum of one adult can remain at the activity the whole time.

Involve a group of children in helping you to cover the table with paper. Show the children the magazines and talk with them about their favourite pages. Encourage the children to talk with each other.

Introduce felt pens and scissors. Children like to cut out pictures and stick them on the table, stick stickers on the paper, write and draw in the magazines, draw their favourite characters on the paper and even copy words or have a go at writing their own words. Take photos of the children mark making and talking with each other for use in follow-up activities.

Follow-up activity: making a wall display

When the activity is finished, carefully remove the paper from the table and trim any tattered edges. You will probably find a large blank space where the children kept the containers of felt pens! Print off the photos and talk to the children about what they had been doing when the photo was taken, e.g. 'I drew Bob the Builder' or 'I wrote *Dora*'. Write down what the children say. Later, draw and cut out a large speech bubble for each child you spoke with. Write their words inside the speech bubbles and attach them to the photos. With the children, stick the photos and speech bubbles in the middle of the paper. Display the paper on the wall with a caption explaining what you were doing and why it was important, e.g. 'Cutting and sticking, and drawing and writing with magazines helps us learn to write!' Put up the display where children and adults can see it. This will help parents understand your approach to early writing and might encourage them to do similar activities at home.

Resources needed

A roll of lining paper to cover a table; masking tape; thick and thin felt pens in containers; a small selection of children's magazines bought from local shops; scissors; glue sticks

Suggested vocabulary

Cut; stick; share; take turns; think about; decide; draw; write; copy

Making Books

Key ideas and activities

Children of all ages enjoy making marks in simple books that either they or the adults have made. If you make a book with blank pages with a child, rather than make one beforehand for them to use, they will be much more likely to talk about what you are doing together, and about what they will draw or write in it when it is finished. It is also useful to have a supply of books that have been made up in advance. These can be placed on a tray in the mark-making area or nearby for the children to help themselves.

Show children how to make different types of books to write in, or encourage them to come up with their own ideas. Make your own book and write and draw in it to act as a role model.

Types of books

Concertina – using half a piece of A4 paper or card cut lengthways. Fold the paper evenly several times, so that it opens up like a concertina. This encourages children to write or draw on each one of the small pages you have made.

Long and thin – made with thin offcuts stapled together, with card front and back covers.

Very small – with a sheet of A4 paper folded three times to make eight pages and four times to make 16 pages. Do this with the children and show them how to fold the paper and cut along the folds that they have made. Make a card cover of the same shape and size for the front and back, then staple the book together.

Very big – with sheets of A3 paper or large sheets of sugar paper.

Shaped – e.g. a circle book with circular pages and covers. Children can draw round plates and other circular objects to make the outline of the circle before they cut out each page. These types of books encourage children to make circular shapes and patterns like spirals.

Younger children will be content to make marks on the pages, perhaps with a different coloured pen on each page. Older children often make up a story and have a go at writing it, or draw a picture on the cover and each page, and possibly have a go at writing (see page 29 *Developmental Writing*).

Resources needed

Offcuts of paper and card; staplers; hole-punches; scissors; rulers; paper clips; treasury tags; sticky tape (clear or masking tape); sugar paper or card for making front and back covers

Suggested vocabulary

Fold; cut; stick; holes; straight; shapes; long; thin; numbers; how many?

Involving Older Children

Key ideas

Children enjoy the company of older children and often imitate what they do – they copy their language and ideas.

Invite staff and children from the local school to visit. Set up mark-making activities that the older children can help the younger ones with. There are also advantages for the older children who can practise some of the skills they have learned in school, e.g. using their 'best handwriting'. They can make story books for the staff and children in your setting to share, and your children can write thank you letters in return. Older brothers and sisters particularly enjoy spending time with their younger siblings, and this can encourage all the children to write and make marks at home.

Activities

Suggestions of activities which older children can help with include:

- making letter shapes and children's names out of play dough
- making books, and drawing and writing short stories
- painting
- drawing with chalk on the ground
- making shapes in the sand tray for the younger children to copy
- making large dice using play dough and the end of a paintbrush to encourage children's mark making and number writing. Younger children can throw the dice and older children can show the younger ones how to make numbers out of play dough and write numbers.

Shapes and pattern cards

Encourage the older children to make shapes and patterns on the table using sand, flour, sugar, rice or beans. Alternatively, using wooden and plastic tools they can cut shapes and patterns into a rectangle of modelling clay. Take photos of the designs, print them on paper and trim to 6 x 4 cm. The child who made each pattern then draws a series of repeated patterns, based on their original design, on the back of the photo. When these are all done the set is laminated.

Give the cards to the children in your setting to encourage them to draw similar patterns and to make their own designs. This also provides a stimulating activity for the older children, and particularly those who may need extra practice with their fine-motor activities.

Talking with Parents

Key ideas and activities

You may know what terms such as *mark making, pincer grasp* or *upper and lower case* mean, but parents are often confused by technical language and might feel put off about discussing their child's progress. I recommend that you use everyday language when talking about mark making. For example, it is helpful to talk about 'pre-writing skills' and 'pretending to write' rather than telling parents about their child's 'fine-motor skills', 'hand-eye coordination' and ability to 'role-play at being a writer'. This also applies to how we write about children's skills and abilities in observations and reports.

Making technical language understandable

With your colleagues, re-write these statements about children's mark making so that they are simple, but accurate. You can use the glossary to help you.

- Mario is beginning to establish his laterality.
- Janine now uses a mature tripod grasp.
- Connor engages in spontaneous developmental writing and makes marks that resemble cursive script.

Talking about children's mark making

Choose a painting or photo of a child involved in early writing. Imagine you are explaining to a parent what this picture tells us about:

- what the child knows
- what the child can do
- how this is relevant for writing.

Talking about movements needed for writing

Do the same as above, using a photo of a child involved in an activity that develops fine-motor or gross-motor skills needed for writing, e.g. squashing play dough, pulling on a rope, using tweezers to pick up small objects or threading beads onto a string.

Writing observations or reports

Look at an observation that you have written about a child's mark making. If you use technical terms like 'fine motor' or 'pincer grasp', can you translate this into plain English?

Talking with parents about their own handwriting

Some parents write only using capital letters (particularly if English is an additional language), while some mix upper case and lower case in the same word. This can cause children to become confused when parents are teaching their children to write their name at home. A positive way to approach parents about this issue is to thank parents for helping their children at home and show the parents their child's name card (see page 31). Explain why you use this particular script and suggest they use this script at home. Photocopy their child's name card and give it to the parents to take home.

Planning a Mark-Making Week

Key ideas

Spend a week focusing on activities that stimulate mark making and early writing. These can be a mixture of successful activities that you already offer, as well as new ideas. This helps to remind colleagues of the many activities you already involve children with that develop mark-making skills. Choose activities from this book and ideas from other settings that you would like to try out. Practise these activities to make sure you have the right resources and to adapt them a little to meet the needs of your children.

Invite parents to stay and take part in activities throughout the week, but plan for a special mark making and early writing open day, when all parents are invited to visit and join in. To prepare for the week, list of all the activities you provide as part of your regular daily practice that stimulate mark making and early writing. Take photos of children involved in these activities. Stick each photo to an A4 piece of card and write a brief description (in plain English!) of how this activity helps early writing. Laminate the cards and display them near the areas where children take part in these activities. Parents can look at these cards as they play with the children. For example:

- 'Climbing on the climbing frame makes my shoulders, arms and hand grip strong.'
- 'Playing with dough helps me talk about what I can do with my hands and learn about shapes. It helps me control what I can do with my fingers.'
- 'Singing songs like *1, 2, 3, 4, 5, Once I Caught a Fish Alive* helps me learn about numbers, my fingers and my left and right hands.'

Activities

Suggested activities might include:
- creating a new writing area with the children
- creating a role-play area, e.g. a Post Office
- having a grand opening of your new mark-making area
- choosing a book that stimulates the children to make patterns and shapes, e.g. *Hooray for Fish* by Lucy Cousins (Walker Books Ltd). Ask parents to share this with groups of children and make paintings or play dough designs based on the book.

Many parents enjoy singing with their children but might not be familiar with the songs you sing with the children. Teach parents the words and actions, perhaps as part of a big sing song on your open day. Invite staff from local schools, other settings and local early years advisors to visit throughout the week and particularly on the open day. Take photos of children taking part in these activities during the week, to use as part of a display and to show parents during an evening to highlight mark making and early writing.

Planning an Event for Parents

Key ideas

Many parents are keen to find about what you do to support early writing and what they can do at home to support you in their work. Inviting them to an evening presentation can be a good way of giving parents information about your work, as well as advice for activities at home. Ask a local early years advisor to help you plan the talk and to support you during your presentation. Give all parents and carers a written invitation well in advance. Keep giving reminders and make sure that they return an RSVP slip to let you know how many people to expect.

When planning a session it is always helpful to meet with your colleagues and discuss your key messages and what the adults will do during the evening – mainly sit, listen and join in a discussion or actually take part in activities?

Key messages

Important messages to cover in the session would include:

- the stages that children pass through and the skills children need to learn to write their name. Include photos of children taking part in activities that help this process
- how your work is similar to all other early years settings in the country (following for example, the English Early Years Foundation Stage curriculum)
- what parents can do at home.

For the event, set the room out showing it ready for the next day. Point out all the activities that you do that support early writing. Allow the parents to take part in some of the activities themselves, e.g. squeezing plastic bottles in the water, making shapes in the sand and with play dough. You could also give the parents a recipe sheet for play dough to make at home.

Most discussions at parents' evenings are likely to revolve around helping children learn to write, including their name. It will be very important to be clear about what your message will be about what you expect children to be able to do, how you and your colleagues look closely at how children are making progress, and when you decide to support children with writing.

If you are able to make positive links with your local school, invite a member of staff to the talk to give a short presentation about how your work supports children when they enter school. If you are part of a school, arrange for one of your teaching colleagues to support you in your planning and during the evening.

Glossary

Automatic movement or action – a movement made without thinking. Many of these movements have been learned by children and repeated so many times that they no longer need to think about them.

Capital letters (also known as upper case) – 'YES' is written in upper case, while 'yes' is in lower case.

Conscious movement or action – a movement made while the child is thinking about it. Children make conscious movements when they are learning a new skill, e.g. doing up a zip. Once they have mastered the skill it becomes automatic.

Copying – when a child tries to do exactly what an adult has done, e.g. write a number correctly.

Copy writing – a technique that adults use to teach children how to orientate letters correctly. Children either copy underneath or on top of what adults have written.

Cursive script – a style of writing where letters are linked together to form whole words or parts of words. Sometimes known as 'joined-up writing'.

Developmental (Emergent) Writing – the stage that children go through when they begin to experiment with making shapes that look like letters, words and numbers. They often do this while role playing writing.

Down syndrome – a genetic condition where children are very likely to have some degree of learning difficulty.

Dyslexia – a learning difficulty that affects children's ability to read and spell. Other difficulties can include sequencing and handwriting (particularly orientation of letters).

Dyspraxia – a disorder of movement where children are often able to make movements automatically but have difficulty when thinking about how to make movements. This can affect speech, gross-motor and fine-motor movements.

Fine-motor movements/skills – actions that involve the muscles that control smaller movements, e.g. using our hands and fingers.

Font – a style of writing on computers and used in printing, e.g. for printing captions for displays.

Forefinger – the finger next to the thumb, also known as the index finger.

Global developmental disability – a long-term learning difficulty. Children make progress with support, but they are likely to have a degree of life-long additional learning need that can involve speech and language, motor, social and emotional and learning difficulties.

Gross-motor movements/skills – actions that involve the muscles that control larger movements of arms, legs and feet, such as swinging arms or kicking a ball. They can also involve the whole body, e.g. running and jumping.

Hand-eye coordination – the ability for our eyes to give the brain information to control and guide our hands to make a coordinated movement, such as catching a ball or writing a letter or number correctly.

Handwriting – how we form letters to write. There are many different styles of handwriting, including printing and cursive script.

Imitation – when children copy adults' behaviour, usually in role play.

Laterality – the preference that most people have to use automatically a hand, arm, leg, foot and eye from one side of the body.

Lower case – letters also known as 'small letters'. The word 'yes' is in lower case, while 'YES' is in upper case.

Manual dexterity – the ability to grasp and use an object in the way that you want to.

Orientation (letter orientation) – the direction we move a pencil or pen when we are writing letters or numbers. Children usually begin to orientate their letters and numbers in their own way, and are then taught correct orientation.

Palmar grasp – using a pencil or paintbrush by holding it with the whole hand.

Pincer grasp – holding an object between the forefinger and thumb.

Posture – the position of a person's body when standing or sitting.

Printing – a handwriting style where individual letters are written without being joined together.

Proprioception – the ability to interpret messages that your body gives you about your position, movement, and balance. The sense of proprioception helps us to be able to make movements without looking, e.g. clapping our hands with our eyes closed or touching a part of our body.

Reflex actions – an action that happens automatically and immediately in response to a stimulus, e.g. moving a hand away quickly after touching something hot. Newborn babies are born with several reflex actions which eventually either disappear or become consciously controlled.

Reversals – when children write letters and numbers back to front. This is a stage that many children go through as they learn and practise correct formation and orientation of letters and numbers.

Role-play writing – when children pretend to write. This can be in role play, such as pretending to be a doctor.

Scribbling – making marks in a random way that have no apparent meaning, but are made for the pleasure children get from doing it.

Tripod grasp (dynamic tripod grasp) – the generally agreed way that children should hold a pen or pencil to write, between thumb, index finger and middle finger.

Upper case – letters also known as 'capital letters'. The word 'YES' is written in upper case.

Visual scanning – moving our eyes to follow an object's movement. When reading English single words and sentences, we visually scan from left to right.

Useful Resources

Available from Yellow Door

Yellow Door publish a range of sensory resources to develop children's understanding of shapes and patterns. The following sets of stones can be hidden in sand or water to develop children's sense of touch, and used in a wide range of sensory play and mark-making activities. Available sets include:

Sensory Stones – Set of 8 stones with four raised designs (circles, dots, wavy lines and a grid) and four indented designs (circles, lines, zigzags and a spiral).

Interlocking Sensory Stones – Set of 8 stones designed in pairs that connect into each other in different ways.

Sensory Shapes – Set of 12 stones including two thicknesses and sizes for each of the six shapes: circle, square, triangle, rectangle, pentagon and hexagon.

Feels-Write Letter Stones are a range of tactile resources which enable children to develop their fine-motor control, the language to talk about shapes and patterns and to practise letter formation. Each stone is carefully engraved so children can trace their finger around the shape – over and over again – building their confidence and memory of how their hand moves to form the letters correctly. The stones are made from a durable mix and are suitable for use across the early years environment, including sand and water play, and outdoors. Available sets include:
Feels-Write Pre-Writing Stones – Set of 12 stones
Feels-Write Lower-Case Letters – Set of 26 stones
Feels-Write Upper-Case Letters – Set of 26 stones
Feels-Write Number Stones – Set of 10 stones

Farmyard Footprints – a set of 8 stones showing an animal on one side and their footprint on the other. They are ideal to use with play dough and for the children to lay footprint trails from left to right.

Also available: *Alphabet Pathway Mats* – a set of 26 mats, ideal for introducing letters and sounds to young children. Each lower case letter is shown clearly with formation arrows. The surrounding artwork is filled with objects starting with the same letter, providing great opportunities for language development. The cards are made from plastic and so are durable for outdoor use.

A wide range of other resources to help develop sensory play, fine-motor skills and early understanding of letters and sounds is also available from Yellow Door: 01223 328051 www.yellow-door.net

We hope you have found this publication useful. Other Lawrence Educational books by Michael Jones are:

Let's Get Talking!	Exciting Ways to Help Children with Speech and Language Difficulties	978-1-903670-88-0
Let's Talk About Maths!	Exciting Ways to Develop Children's Language and Love of Maths from an Early Age	978-1-903670-92-7
Supporting Quiet Children	Exciting Ideas and Activities to Help Reluctant Talkers Become Confident Talkers	978-1-903670-90-3

You may also like our *50 Exciting Ideas* series:

Builder's Tray	50 Exciting Ways to Use a Builder's Tray	978-1-903670-15-6
Let's Build	50 Exciting Ideas for Construction Play	978-1-903670-30-9
Let's Explore!	50 Exciting Starting Points for Science Activities	978-1-903670-11-8
Let's Take a Story Book Outside	Exciting Ways to Promote Outdoor Creativity	978-1-903670-76-7
Let's Talk Behaviour!	50 Inclusive Ideas to Support Effective Communication and Understanding	978-1-903670-93-4
Let's Write!	50 Exciting Starting Points for Writing Experiences	978-1-903670-10-1
Literacy Outdoors	50 Exciting Starting Points for Outdoor Literacy Experiences	978-1-903670-53-8
Maths Outdoors	50 Exciting Ways to Develop Mathematical Awareness Outdoors	978-1-903670-61-3
Maths Through Stories	50 Exciting Ideas for Developing Maths Through Stories	978-1-903670-46-0
Mud Kitchens and Beyond	50 Exciting Ideas for Investigative Play	978-1-903670-96-5
Nursery Rhymes	50 Nursery Rhymes to Play With	978-1-903670-23-1
Plant an Idea	50 Exciting Ways to Use Flowers, Trees and Plant Life Throughout the Year	978-1-903670-24-8
Science Outdoors	50 Exciting Ways for Children to Explore the World Around Them	978-1-903670-67-5
Storyboxes	50 Exciting Ideas for Storyboxes	978-1-903670-16-3
Superheroes and Popular Culture	50 Exciting Ideas for Using Superheroes and Popular Culture	978-1-903670-79-8
The Small World Recipe Book	50 Exciting Ideas for Small World Play	978-1-903670-39-2
Things to Do Outside	50 Exciting Things to Do Outside	978-1-903670-07-1
This is the Way I Like to Play	50 Exciting Ideas to Support Investigative Play through Schemas	978-1-903670-95-8

For further information about these and our other publications, visit our website:
www.LawrenceEducational.co.uk